GLOBAL RECESSION - CAUSES, IMPACTS AND REMEDIES

AFTER THE FINANCIAL CRISIS

ANALYSES OF KEY POLICY RESPONSES AND ECONOMIC RECOVERY

GLOBAL RECESSION - CAUSES, IMPACTS AND REMEDIES

Additional books in this series can be found on Nova's website under the Series tab.

Additional E-books in this series can be found on Nova's website under the E-book tab.

GLOBAL RECESSION - CAUSES, IMPACTS AND REMEDIES

AFTER THE FINANCIAL CRISIS

ANALYSES OF KEY POLICY RESPONSES AND ECONOMIC RECOVERY

EDGAR I. BAIR
EDITOR

New York

For permission to use material from this book please contact us:
Telephone 631-231-7269; Fax 631-231-8175
Web Site: http://www.novapublishers.com

Additional color graphics may be available in the e-book version of this book.

LIBRARY OF CONGRESS CATALOGING-IN-PUBLICATION DATA

ISBN: 978-1-62948-593-5

Published by Nova Science Publishers, Inc. † New York

CONTENTS

PREFACE

This book describes 15 key elements of the response to the financial crises – providing an overview of the state of the economy and the financial system, the actions the Administration took in conjunction with the Federal Reserve and other regulators, and where we are now.

Chapter 1 – Five years ago, a financial crisis unlike any in generations rocked Wall Street, turning a recession that was already hammering Main Street into the worst economic crisis since the Great Depression. In the months before President Obama took office, the economy was shrinking at a rate of over 8%. Businesses were shedding 800,000 jobs a month. Banks had stopped lending to families and small businesses. The iconic American auto industry – the heartbeat of American manufacturing – was on the brink of collapse. It was a crisis that would ultimately cost millions of Americans their jobs, their homes, and their savings – and the decades-long erosion of middle-class security was laid bare for all to see and feel.

President Obama acted quickly to rescue the auto industry, cut taxes for middle-class families, and keep teachers in the classrooms and first responders on our streets. He took on Wall Street, ending taxpayer bailouts, putting in place tough new rules on big banks, and establishing new consumer protections that cracked down on the worst practices of mortgage lenders and credit card companies. He changed a tax code too skewed in favor of the wealthiest Americans, locking in tax cuts for 98% of working Americans, and asked those at the top to pay a little more. And he took on a broken health care system and invested in new American technologies to reverse our addiction to foreign oil.

Chapter 2 – The 2007-2009 recession was long and deep, and according to several indicators was the most severe economic contraction since the 1930s (but still much less severe than the Great Depression). The slowdown of economic activity was moderate through the first half of 2008, but at that point the weakening economy was overtaken by a major financial crisis that would exacerbate the economic weakness and accelerate the decline.

Economic recovery began in mid-2009. Real gross domestic product (GDP) has been on a positive track since then, although the pace has been uneven and slowed significantly in 2011. The stock market has recovered from its lows, and employment has increased moderately. On the other hand, significant economic weakness remains evident, particularly in the balance sheet of households, the labor market, and the housing sector.

Congress was an active participant in the policy responses to this crisis and has an ongoing interest in macroeconomic conditions. Current macroeconomic concerns include whether the economy is in a sustained recovery, rapidly reducing unemployment, speeding a return to normal output and employment growth, and addressing government's long-term debt problem.

In the typical post-war business cycle, lower than normal growth during the recession is quickly followed by a recovery period with above normal growth. This above normal growth serves to speed up the reentry of the unemployed to the workforce. Once the economy reaches potential output (and full employment), growth returns to its normal growth path, where the pace of aggregate spending advances in step with the pace of aggregate supply. There is concern that this time the U.S. economy will either not return to its pre-recession growth path but perhaps remain permanently below it, or return to the pre-crisis path but at a slower than normal pace. Problems on the supply side and the demand side of the economy have so far led to a weaker than normal recovery.

If the pace of private spending proves insufficient to assure a sustained recovery, would further stimulus by monetary and fiscal policy be warranted? One lesson from the Great Depression is to guard against a too hasty withdrawal of fiscal and monetary stimulus in an economy recovering from a deep decline.

The removal of fiscal and monetary stimulus in 1937 is thought to have stopped a recovery and caused a slump that did not end until WWII. Opponents of further stimulus maintain that the accumulation of additional government debt would lower future economic growth, but supporters argue that additional stimulus is the appropriate near-term policy.

Moreover, in 2011-2012, the sharply fading effects of fiscal stimulus and weaker growth in Europe have likely dampened economic growth.

In regard to the long-term debt problem, in an economy operating close to potential output, government borrowing to finance budget deficits will in theory draw down the pool of national saving, crowding out private capital investment and slowing long-term growth. However, the U.S. economy is currently operating well short of capacity and the risk of such crowding out occurring is therefore low in the near term. Once the cyclical problem of weak demand is resolved and the economy has returned to a normal growth path, mainstream economists' consensus policy response for an economy with a looming debt crisis is fiscal consolidation—cutting deficits.

Such a policy would have the benefits of low and stable interest rates, a less fragile financial system, improved investment prospects, and possibly faster long-term growth.

Chapter 3 – The pace of economic recovery from the 2007-2009 recession has been historically slow. Over four years of recovery, the annual rate of growth of real gross domestic product (GDP) has averaged 2%, well below the 3% to 5% typical of other post-WWII recoveries. As a result, the output gap—the difference between what the economy could produce and what it actually produced—has only declined from a high of 8.1% in mid-2009 to a still large 5.8% in mid- 2013. Slow growth of output has translated into a slow reduction of unemployment.

The recovery has persisted, in part, due to support to aggregate spending by policies of fiscal and monetary stimulus. However, fiscal stimulus has steadily dissipated since 2010 and in 2013 the federal budget has turned contractionary. While monetary policy is expected to remain stimulative through 2013, it is unlikely to add to that stimulus to counteract the increasing drag of falling federal budget deficits on economic activity. Therefore, sustaining the recovery's momentum in the remainder of 2013 and into 2014 may require a greater push from private spending, particularly household consumption spending.

In the aftermath of the 2007-2009 recession, which involved a substantial loss of net worth and increase in the burden of debt, households' actions to repair their severely damaged balance sheets by reducing debt and building wealth is thought by many economists to be a key factor dissipating the strength of consumer spending. Although this repair is necessary for building a stronger economy in the long run, it has slowed the economy-wide recovery and job creation in the short run.

Where households currently stand in repairing their balance sheets is likely to influence the strength of consumer spending going forward. If substantially complete, it would point to the prospect of stronger consumer spending and increased momentum of the economic recovery; but if substantial wealth building is still needed, it would diminish that prospect.

A number of indicators paint a mixed picture of the prospect for stronger consumer spending. Despite clear progress, more repair of the severely damaged household balance sheet may be needed before households begin to spend at a faster pace. The typical household has likely only seen modest improvement in its net worth in large measure because the value of real estate, most often the largest asset it holds, has only recently been increasing. The rebound of the housing market portends progress for the typical household rebuilding its wealth, but it is unlikely that this process will be completed in 2013, making it also likely that tepid spending by consumers will continue.

Determining the state of household net worth has implications for the optimal policy response going forward. If household net worth is judged to have not fully recovered from the damage incurred in 2007-2009, particularly for the typical household, some may regard this as an indicator of a continuing need for macroeconomic policy to provide stimulus to maintain the recovery's upward momentum. It could also have implications for federal policy measures that are aimed at providing direct help in removing the burden of household debt through programs that restructure mortgage debt.

In: After the Financial Crisis
Editor: Edgar I. Bair
ISBN: 978-1-62948-593-5

Chapter 1

THE FINANCIAL CRISIS: FIVE YEARS LATER*

National Economic Council, The President's Council of Economic Advisers, The Domestic Policy Council and The Office of Management and Budget

EXECUTIVE SUMMARY

Five years ago, a financial crisis unlike any in generations rocked Wall Street, turning a recession that was already hammering Main Street into the worst economic crisis since the Great Depression. In the months before President Obama took office, the economy was shrinking at a rate of over 8%. Businesses were shedding 800,000 jobs a month. Banks had stopped lending to families and small businesses. The iconic American auto industry – the heartbeat of American manufacturing – was on the brink of collapse. It was a crisis that would ultimately cost millions of Americans their jobs, their homes, and their savings – and the decades-long erosion of middle-class security was laid bare for all to see and feel.

President Obama acted quickly to rescue the auto industry, cut taxes for middle-class families, and keep teachers in the classrooms and first responders

* This report was released by the Executive Office of the President, September 2013.

on our streets. He took on Wall Street, ending taxpayer bailouts, putting in place tough new rules on big banks, and establishing new consumer protections that cracked down on the worst practices of mortgage lenders and credit card companies. He changed a tax code too skewed in favor of the wealthiest Americans, locking in tax cuts for 98% of working Americans, and asked those at the top to pay a little more. And he took on a broken health care system and invested in new American technologies to reverse our addiction to foreign oil.

Five years later, America has fought our way back. Because of these tough choices, over the past three and a half years, our businesses have created seven and a half million new jobs. Manufacturers are adding jobs for the first time since the mid-1990's. We generate more renewable energy than ever, and our exports are at all-time highs. Health care costs are growing at the slowest rate in 50 years – and our deficit has fallen by 50% since the President took office.

Thanks to the grit and resilience of the American people, we've cleared away the rubble from the financial crisis and begun to lay a new foundation for stronger, more durable economic growth. And the last thing we can afford right now is a decision from a minority of Republicans in Congress to throw our economy back into crisis by refusing to pay our country's bills or shutting down the government. As President Obama has said, we're not where we need to be yet – the challenges facing the middle class weren't created overnight, and they won't be solved overnight. That's why we need to keep building on that foundation by focusing on the cornerstones of a strong, secure middle-class life: a good job, a quality education, a home of your own, affordable health care when you need it, and a secure retirement. That's the conviction that has driven President Obama since he first ran for this office – that our economy works best when it grows not from the top-down, but from the middle-class out – that we are stronger when everyone who works hard has a chance to get ahead.

This report describes 15 key elements of the response to the financial crises – providing an overview of the state of the economy and the financial system, the actions the Administration took in conjunction with the Federal Reserve and other regulators, and where we are now:

I. The Administration's Responded to the Crisis With Speed and Comprehensiveness: Within six months of taking office, President Obama had acted with nearly unprecedented speed and force, by taking the following key actions:

- Signing the Recovery Act into law within 30 days of taking office
- Announcing a framework for a new financial stability plan within three weeks of taking office
- Implementing the key steps of that plan within four months of taking office, including the stress test, new housing measures, support for small businesses and small banks and efforts to restart securities markets that support consumer lending
- Taking action to support the American automotive industry within five months of taking office

II. The Administration's Efforts Stabilized the Financial System While Recovering Taxpayers' Investments: When President Obama took office, the financial system was still on the brink, despite the initial implementation of the Troubled Asset Relief Program (TARP). Upon taking office, the President continued to use TARP resources to support our financial system, but also meaningfully expanded its use to help millions of families impacted by the housing crisis, restructure the auto industry and support small businesses.

- ***The Federal Government Is Expected to Receive a Profit on the Response to the Financial Crisis:*** While initial estimates by the Congressional Budget Office projected the TARP program would cost over $350 billion, Treasury has already received nearly $422 billion in total cash payments back from the government's investments in TARP and support for AIG, more than the $421 billion it disbursed through TARP – with further repayments expected. Broader measures of the Federal government's response to the crisis also project that the government will receive an overall profit.

III. Treasury Has More Than Recovered Its Investments in Banks: Treasury aggressively managed the TARP bank investment portfolio in a manner that balanced the desire to exit these investments as soon as possible with the goal of maximizing returns for taxpayers.

- ***Federal Government Has Made a Nearly $28 Billion Return on TARP Bank Investments:*** Despite initial fears that TARP investments in banks would cost taxpayers hundreds of billions of dollars, Treasury has recovered $28 billion more than was disbursed on its bank investments so far – receiving $273 billion back after investing

$245 billion – while achieving the original policy goals of stabilizing the banks and preserving lending.

IV. Stress Tests Built Confidence in the Banking System without Putting New Taxpayer Funds at Risk: In February 2009, the Administration and the Federal bank regulators announced comprehensive stress tests of the nation's largest banks to reduce uncertainty regarding their solvency, help stabilize the financial system, and ensure they were able to continue lending.

- ***The Stress Tests Resulted in the Banks Raising More than $80 Billion in New Private Capital Without Additional Government Support:*** Within months of the release of the results, the largest banks in the country raised over $80 billion of equity capital from private sources, with no major banks requiring additional government support outside General Motors Acceptance Corporation's (GMAC) participation in the auto program.
- ***Stress Tests Are Now a Model in the United States and Around the World:*** Today, stress tests modeled after the crisis-era stress tests have been adopted as part of the regular supervisory framework in the United States, and stress tests have been adopted as a norm in the global regulatory community.

V. The Government Has Achieved a Profit on Its Investments in AIG: After intervening to stabilize AIG during the financial crisis to prevent a greater shock through the global economy, the Administration took immediate steps to restructure AIG and accelerate the timeline for AIG's repayment of the government's support.

- **Rather than Lose Tens of Billions of Dollars, the Government Turned a $22.7 Billion Return on Its Investments in AIG:** Despite widespread predictions that the American taxpayers stood to lose billions on its $182.3 billion of assistance to AIG, the Administration successfully recouped $205 billion, for a total positive return to the taxpayers of $22.7 billion, and AIG's loan to the Federal Reserve was fully repaid.

VI. The Auto Industry Is Growing Again: When President Obama took office, the auto industry was on the brink of collapse – and as access to credit for car loans dried up, auto sales plunged by 40 percent. The Administration promptly took key steps to stabilize the auto industry and return it to viability.

- ***The American Auto Industry Is Profitable, Gaining Market Share, and Creating Jobs Again:*** Over 1 million people are working in the auto industry as a direct result of the auto rescue, according to the non-partisan Center for Automotive Research. Today, the Big Three are profitable and gaining market share for first time in 20 years. Auto sales were higher in August than any month in over 6 years. The auto industry is creating jobs at the fastest pace in 15 years, with over 340,000 jobs created since June 2009 when GM and Chrysler emerged from bankruptcy.
- ***American Taxpayers are Being Paid Back Significantly More Than Expected.*** Despite the chorus of warnings that the government would not recoup the vast majority of its investments in the auto companies, American taxpayers are seeing progress, having recovered 90% of the total invested in Chrysler and a substantial portion of its investments in GM. Ally, formerly known as GMAC, also recently announced a plan to pay the government back another $6 billion; Treasury is continuing to work with the company to recover its remaining investment.

VII. The President's Policies Supported Homeowners and Helped Heal Our Housing Market: To stabilize the housing market and help families avoid foreclosure, the President took bold action through an array of programs.

- ***The President's Efforts Have Helped Nearly 7 Million Families Modify their Mortgages and 2.7 Million More Refinance Their Mortgages:*** Among other programs, the President launched the Home Affordable Modification Program (HAMP), which has led to 7 million households getting government and private sector relief, and Home Affordable Refinancing Program (HARP), a refinancing program that nearly tripled in volume after further changes to the program, rising from 400,000 homeowners in 2011 to 1.1 million in 2012, helping over 2.7 million in total.
- ***The Housing Market Is Now Coming Back, with Prices Increasing 12% in the Last Year:*** Today, the housing market is coming back thanks in part to the extensive measures taken by the President. House prices have been rising at the fastest pace in seven years, resulting in 5

million homeowners coming out from underwater in the last six quarters. The President continues to fight for additional measures to ensure every responsible family has a fair shot to refinance and no community is left behind by the recovery.

VIII. The Obama Administration's Efforts Supported Small Business: With small businesses struggling from an inability to access credit, the Administration took action to support small businesses.

- ***The Administration Provided Critical Support for Small Businesses:*** Among many other steps, the Administration provided capital to small banks, backstopped liquidity in the market for SBA loans and passed a Small Business Jobs Act that included tax relief and supported access to credit for entrepreneurs. While much has been accomplished, there is more to do to ensure small businesses continue to have broad access to credit and that they remain the engine of growth for our economy.

IX. Immediate Action Helped Restart the Flow of Credit to American Families: When capital markets froze and funding dried up, banks reduced lending to consumers and businesses to conserve liquidity. By unfreezing securities markets that play a crucial role in consumer and business lending, the Administration's response unclogged the credit pipes of the financial system.

- ***Consumers Are Better Able to Access Affordable Credit:*** Since the recession, the price of auto loans and credit card borrowing has improved substantially and banks have begun easing their lending standards, while also reporting stronger consumer demand in most loan categories.

X. Household Wealth Has Begun to Recover: As a result of the financial crisis, household wealth fell by $19 trillion — with the value of retirement accounts alone dropping $2.8 trillion between September 2007 and December 2008. While many families still have not recovered from the impact of the financial crisis, the Administration's response has helped start putting families on the road to recovery.

- ***Americans have Recovered Nearly $15 Trillion in Household Net Worth:*** Although there is still far to go to recover from the impact of the financial crisis and progress has been uneven so far, by the end of 2012, Americans had recovered $14.7 trillion of aggregate household net worth, recouping 91% of the recession losses.

XI. The Strongest Consumer Financial Protections in History Are Being Implemented: The financial crisis demonstrated one of the most glaring gaps in our regulatory framework – the absence of a watchdog agency to protect consumers for consumer financial products and services. The President fought for and signed into law the strongest consumer financial protections in history with the Dodd-Frank Wall Street Reform and Consumer Protection Act, which created the Consumer Financial Protection Bureau (CFPB) and tasked it with one job: to protect families when they make important financial decisions.

- ***Substantial New Consumer Protections Have Been Rolled Out:*** The Bureau has already launched a number of new requirements and initiatives to ensure that mortgage and other consumer lending processes are transparent and straightforward, and empower consumers with the financial information necessary for borrowing decisions.

XII. Financial Reform Has Helped Rein in Excessive Risk-Taking: In the run-up to the financial crisis, many of the largest banks took on excessive risks without appropriate safeguards, while large-scale bank-like activities outside the regulated banking system grew significantly.

- ***Wall Street Reform is Closing Gaps in Regulation:*** Reforms put the toughest standards on the largest firms, directly limit interconnectedness, and allow regulators to identify risks building up outside of the banking system. In addition, many of the elements of the "shadow banking" system have become smaller and pose less risk. The impact of these reforms underscore the importance of finishing the work of Dodd-Frank implementation to ensure that the mistakes of the Great Recession never occur again.

XIII. New Tools Have Been Put in Place to Ensure the Failure of a Large, Interconnected Firm No Longer Puts the System at Risk: When the financial crisis hit, regulators lacked effective tools to resolve large failing firms. Key reforms will help ensure no institution is "too big to fail."

- ***Large Institutions File "Living Wills" and Won't Be Bailed Out Again:*** Large banks and designated firms are now required to create "living wills" to provide a roadmap for resolving the firm through bankruptcy, and new tools are now available to orderly and responsibly resolve failed financial institutions. Internationally, regulators have worked together to align standards and coordinate actions in the event of the failure of a large global firm

XIV. Banks Are Significantly Better Capitalized – Making Them Better Able to Withstand Future Shocks: The crisis proved that most banks maintained an unacceptably low cushion of Tier 1 capital – a measure of high quality, loss-absorbing capital.

- ***Bank Capital Has More Than Doubled:*** As a result of new bank capital standards and the stress tests, bank capital has doubled from a Tier 1 common equity ratio of 5.6 percent to 11.1 percent over the last five years, substantially increasing the stability of the U.S. banking system. Banks now hold sufficient capital so that, even under adverse stress test scenarios, they would hold more of it than their actual capital levels in 2008.

XV. Wall Street Reform Has Reduced Risk in the Derivatives Market: To address the risks posed by derivatives, the President pushed for fundamental domestic and international reforms to strengthen the derivatives market and oversight of its participants.

- ***Wall Street Reform Addresses Risks from Derivatives:*** The Dodd-Frank Act establishes requirements for major swap dealers and participants to be subject to greater supervision, and requires standardized OTC derivatives to be traded on swap execution facilities and centrally cleared, and for data to be reported to repositories to increase transparency and price discovery.

I. SPEED AND COMPREHENSIVENESS OF CRISIS RESPONSE

Five Years Ago

- **In 2008, the American economy was on the brink of collapse**. In the autumn of 2008, the American financial system was teetering on the edge, with numerous banks and other financial institutions failing, auto companies struggling, the housing market in free fall, and the economy in a severe downturn.
- **The American economy had not faced such a severe economic downturn since the Great Depression.** Job losses averaged nearly 800,000 per month between November 2008 and April 2009 as the unemployment rate climbed substantially. The economy contracted at a staggering rate of 8.3% between the 4th quarter of 2008 and the 1st quarter of 2009, and the Dow fell as low as 6,400 in March of 2009. Middle class families were hit hard, losing $7 trillion in homeowners' equity by January 2009 due to plummeting home prices and $19 trillion of household wealth. Millions lost their homes to foreclosure, while consumers and businesses lost access to credit.
- **Though several specific events triggered the financial crisis, it was years in the making.** Though the financial crisis came to a head in September 2008 with the failure of Lehman Brothers, the primary causes of the crisis had been building for years, including predatory lending by many lenders, reckless business models on Wall Street, excessive financial leverage, increased complexity through existing and new channels like structured products and derivatives, and an outdated regulatory system.
- **The financial crisis took a huge toll on middle class families and Main Street**. Families suffered from falling home prices, retirement savings were wiped out, and qualified borrowers had trouble getting access to student, auto, and consumer loans as well as mortgages. Meanwhile, both small businesses and larger corporations found their access to financing cut-off, often unable to invest in growth or access working capital.
- **Along with the Federal Reserve and the FDIC, the Bush Administration had taken a number of key steps in response to the deepening crisis – including its successful proposal to Congress for $700 billion in rescue funding and subsequent investment in the banks – but the system still remained on the**

brink. Support from the Federal Reserve's liquidity facilities to various credit markets and the government's support for AIG, loans to the auto companies, and guarantee programs for money market funds and bank debt had been essential but were not sufficient to stabilize the broader system.

Obama Administration Actions

Upon Taking Office, the President Moved with Nearly Unprecedented Speed and Force

- **Signed into law the $800 billion Recovery Act within 30 days of taking office**. With leadership and support from the President, Congress passed the American Recovery and Reinvestment Act, which was signed into law by President Obama on February 17. The Act was necessary to stem the tide as demand in the U.S. and around the world continued to contract.
- **Put in place a comprehensive Financial Stability Plan within four months of taking office – even though it required unprecedented policy actions.** The President announced the framework for his Financial Stability plan within three weeks of taking office, and put in place the major elements shortly thereafter, even though it involved designing and implementing many original but necessary policy interventions.
    - **Stress Test and Capital Assistance Program (CAP):** Treasury and the regulatory agencies announced comprehensive stress tests of the nation's largest banks to reduce uncertainty regarding their solvency and to help stabilize the financial system by requiring banks to raise more capital if they were found to have an insufficient amount of equity. The stress test was designed to ensure that banks had the capital to continue lending even in adverse economic conditions and restore market confidence in the financial system. Treasury also announced a program for those banks found to need additional capital but unable to access the private markets. However, the program was designed to encourage the institutions to replace public assistance with private capital as soon as possible, rather than relying on the government.
    - **Housing**: On February 18, less than a month after taking office, the President launched the Homeowners Affordability and

Stability Plan including the Home Affordable Modification Program (HAMP), which has directly and indirectly helped millions of homeowners avoid foreclosures. At a time when the mortgage industry was ill-equipped to respond adequately to the crisis, the Administration's initiatives introduced important consumer protections for homeowners, setting new industry standards. Recognizing that more Americans could be helped by refinancing, President Obama also worked with independent regulators to set up the Home Affordable Refinancing Program (HARP) and then acted to expand it further when it became clear that more families could benefit.

- **The Term Asset-Backed Securities Loan Facility (TALF):** Treasury, jointly with the Federal Reserve, expanded the TALF program established in November 2008 to offer financing to investors to buy securities backed by student loans, auto loans, and other consumer loans, kick-starting secondary lending markets to bring down borrowing costs and help get credit flowing again. This in turn helped give consumers access to auto and student loans more easily and at more affordable terms.
- **Public-Private Investment Program (PPIP):** This program provided government capital and financing to help leverage private capital to create active markets for the legacy securities and real estate related assets that were at the center of the crisis. By helping to stabilize the market for these assets, PPIP helped contribute to ensuring the broader credit markets remained open for households and businesses.

- **Intervened to save the American auto industry and protect manufacturing, despite vocal opposition from public commentators.** After initially rejecting the companies' viability plans and demanding a more rigorous strategy for recovery, the President ultimately made the tough choice to support the American automotive industry by extending additional financial support.

  Specifically, the Obama Administration committed additional assistance to Chrysler and General Motors contingent on them executing a swift, comprehensive restructuring of their operations, which involved difficult but necessary sacrifices from all involved stakeholders.
- **Supported small businesses.** Small banks, the lifeline of small business credit, needed more focused support. Treasury established

two programs, CPP and CDCI, in 2008 and 2010 to stabilize small and large banks across the country. Over 90% of CPP and CDCI participants were banks with less than $10 billion in assets, nearly 70% were small banks with assets under $1 billion, and the median size of CPP banks was approximately $500 million in assets. The President also supported the creation of new programs, including the Small Business Lending Fund (SBLF) to support bank lending to small business and the State Small Business Credit Initiative (SSBCI) to support state and local programs that make credit available to small businesses.

Five Years Later

- **The unprecedented response to the crisis stabilized our system and set our economy on the path to recovery.** Since the crisis, bank capital is at record highs, credit is flowing again, auto sales are booming, the housing market is recovering, and millions of jobs have been created. While we still have a long way to go to make up lost ground in some key areas, the progress is considerable.
- **To date, Treasury has received more in total cash payments, including AIG proceeds, than the amount it disbursed through TARP, defying the critics' predictions.** Of the $700 billion originally approved for TARP by Congress, as of August 31, 2013, Treasury has disbursed $421 billion. Already, Treasury has received nearly $422 billion in payments recovered on the TARP-related rescue programs together with Treasury's additional proceeds from AIG. Treasury continues to disburse funds related to its housing programs, and recoup additional repayments on its outstanding investments.
- **Through Wall Street Reform, the President has laid the foundation for a better future.** The passage of the Dodd-Frank Act has strengthened the recovery and helped prevent a future crisis, implementing some of the strongest Wall Street reforms and consumer protections in our nation's history.

II. Troubled Asset Relief Program (TARP)

Five Years Ago

- **Over the course of 2007 and 2008, the housing market increasingly weakened, contributing to the failure of Bear Stearns, Fannie Mae, and Freddie Mac.**
- **The failure of Lehman Brothers in September 2008 led to a widespread panic that initially affected Wall Street firms but quickly impacted non-financial businesses as they lost access to funding.** Losses on Lehman debt led to immediate withdrawals from money market mutual funds (MMFs), in turn leading to a contraction in the commercial paper market used by corporations to finance their businesses. Meanwhile, banks saw substantial deposit withdrawals and runs by counterparties, pushing these banks to the brink and threatening broader access to credit.
- **In response to the deepening crisis, Congress approved a Bush Administration proposal for $700 billion in funding to provide extraordinary support to the financial markets and firms.** As the crisis worsened, in October 2008 the Treasury shifted from its proposed focus on buying toxic assets and asked 9 major financial institutions to accept capital injections before announcing a broader $250 billion bank investment program the next day. These investments were then followed by an initial restructuring of the investment in AIG and bridge loans to the automakers.
- **In January 2009, despite the initial round of TARP investments in various sectors and essential liquidity provided to the system by the Federal Reserve, the financial system was still on the brink.** Many observers still believed the banking system was at risk of collapsing, credit markets were largely frozen, the automakers were headed toward an uncontrolled failure, and many other challenges remained.
- **Observers estimated that the cost of the support provided would end up being enormous,** with CBO estimating the cost of TARP would be $356 billion, and many claiming the broader financial rescue would cost in the trillions of dollars.

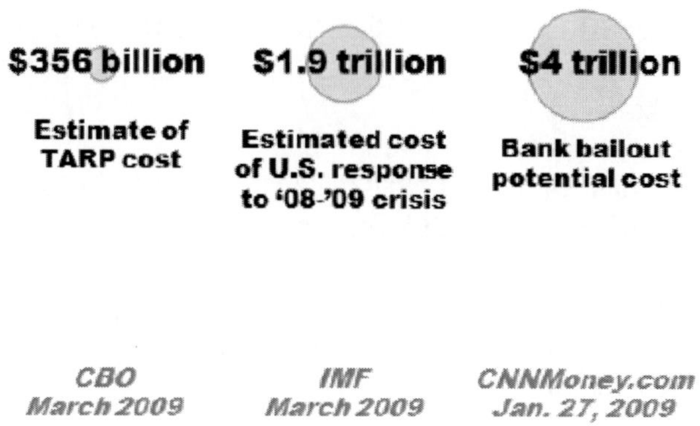

Obama Administration Actions

- **On taking office, the President continued to use TARP resources to support our financial system, but also meaningfully expanded its use to help millions of families impacted by the housing crisis, restructure the auto industry and support small businesses.** The President announced the framework for his Financial Stability plan within three weeks of taking office and put in place the major elements shortly thereafter, including the implementation of many original policy actions. The Financial Stability Plan targeted consumer lending (TALF and PPIP), the stability of the banking sector (the stress tests and CAP), and keeping millions of people in their homes (HAMP and HARP). Other programs later rolled out included support for GM and Chrysler and the Hardest Hit Fund for states most burdened by the housing crisis.
- **By taking such quick action and stabilizing the system, the President helped turn the corner on the crisis and avoided substantial additional costs that could have piled up.**

Five Years Later

- **Taxpayers have already received more in total cash payments (including AIG proceeds) than the amount disbursed through TARP, even though many critics expected TARP to lose hundreds of billions of dollars.** To date, the Government has collected nearly

$422 billion in repayments, dividends, interest, and other income recovered on TARP-related programs and proceeds from the rescue of AIG – compared to $421 billion it has disbursed to date through TARP Treasury is continuing to disburse funds related to its housing programs, while recouping its outstanding investments.

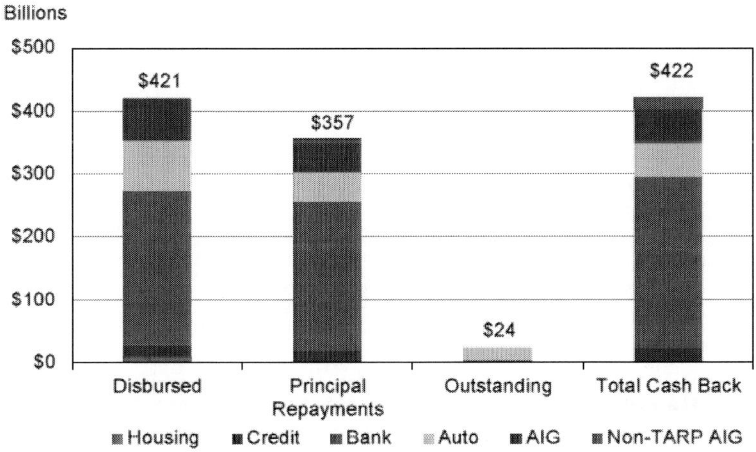

Source: U.S. Department of the Treasury.

Chart 2.1. Disposition of TARP Funds as of August 31, 2013.

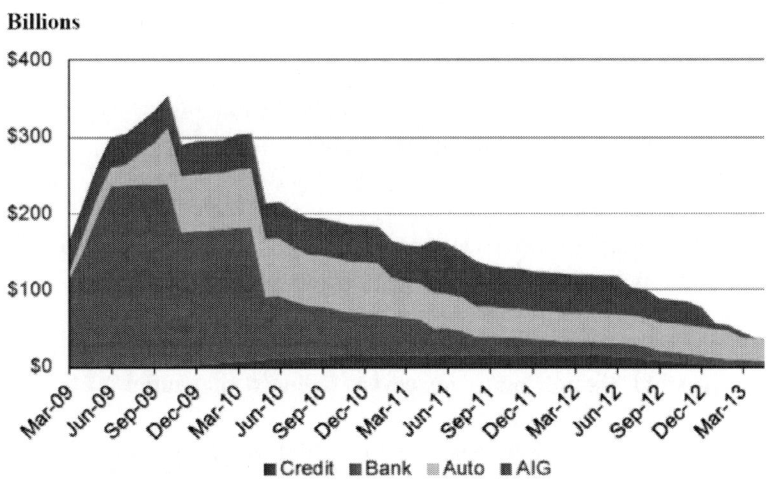

Source: U.S. Department of the Treasury.

Chart 2.2. Total TARP Funds Outstanding.

- **The policies pursued through TARP, along with other extraordinary measures taken by the government and the Federal Reserve, helped stabilize the financial system and facilitate the recovery.** The banking sector was shored up through the bank investment program and the stress tests, while capital has doubled – up nearly $450 billion – and the banks are lending again. The auto sector is thriving again with 340,000 jobs created and 1 million cars and trucks exported in 2012. Housing is recovering, with nearly 7 million helped through modifications and other homeowner assistance actions and home prices up 12 percent year-overyear. And the cost of borrowing for small businesses has fallen for 10 straight quarters and is the lowest since 2009, while more and more lenders are easing borrowing terms for consumers.

III. TARP BANK INVESTMENTS

Five Years Ago

- **In the wake of the collapse of Lehman Brothers on September 15, 2008, numerous large financial institutions faced a "run on the bank" as counterparties refused to extend financing.** Key regulators feared that nearly all of the nation's major financial institutions were at risk of failure within a period of a week or two. In particular, investors and uninsured depositors withdrew tens of billions of dollars from commercial banks of all types, while investors and other market participants withdrew tens of billions of assets in custody from investment banks, leading to a huge net outflow of liquidity from these firms.
- **Reflecting these developments, bank credit spreads widened to all-time highs** and the funding markets began to shut down.
- **The Bush Administration intervened with a round of bank investments through TARP that helped begin to stabilize the system, though many observers believed that much of these bank investments would be lost.**
- **In January 2009, despite the initial efforts, markets remained leery of the continued potential for bank failures,** with continued write-downs and losses at banks unnerving investors and

counterparties and exacerbating the severe funding pressures faced by many institutions.

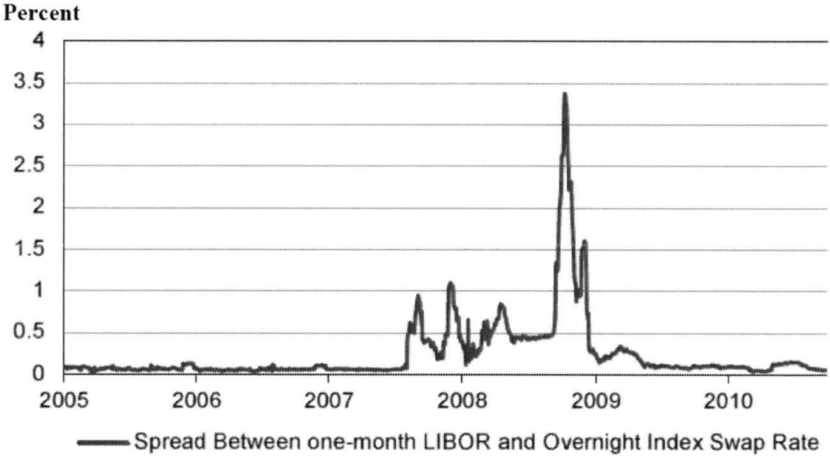

Source: Bloomberg.

Chart 3.1. Cost of Interbank Lending.

Obama Administration Actions

- **In February 2009, the Administration and regulators announced comprehensive stress tests of the nation's largest banks in order to stabilize the banks and help shore up their ability to lend, substantially increasing the effectiveness of the original TARP bank investments.** The stress tests, administered by the Federal Reserve and other bank regulators, included a more adverse economic scenario to help ensure that even under the worst conditions the banks would remain solvent and in a position to continue lending.
- **The Administration aggressively managed the TARP bank investment portfolio in a manner that balanced the desire to exit these investments as soon as possible with the goal of maximizing returns for taxpayers.** Banking investments under TARP were designed to give taxpayers additional returns through the sale of warrants that Treasury received in addition to dividends and interest payments on those investments.

Five Years Later

- **Federal government has made a $28 billion return to date on TARP investments in banks.** Despite initial fears that TARP investments in banks would cost taxpayers hundreds of billions of dollars, as of today, Treasury has recovered $28 billion more than the $245 billion disbursed, collecting $273 billion from TARP bank investments so far. Treasury is continuing to recover funds from the remaining $3.2 billion of bank investments, and every additional dollar collected represents an additional gain for taxpayers.
- **In addition, the combination of the TARP capital support program and the stress test motivated banks to raise significant capital in 2009 through private sources, which helped achieve the original policy goals of stabilizing the banks and preserving bank lending.**
- **Ultimately, TARP's bank programs provided capital to more than 700 banks throughout the country, including more than 450 small, community banks.** These capital injections stabilized these institutions and helped preserve access to credit to the economy.

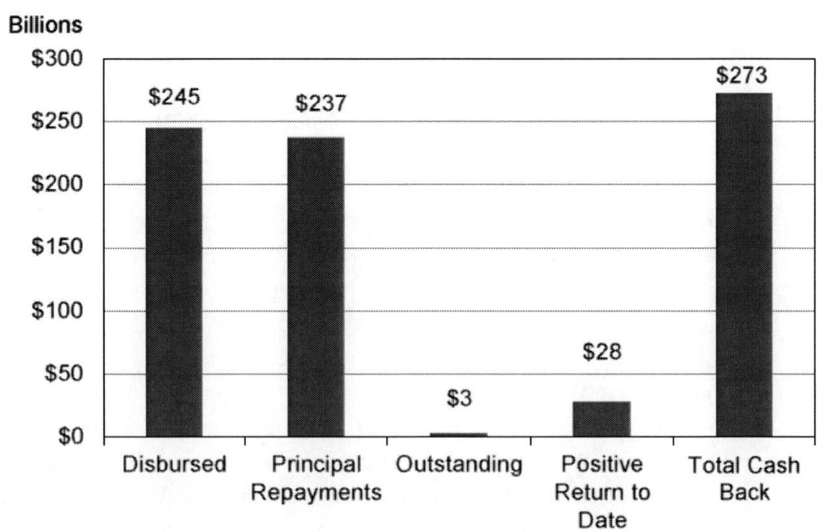

Source: U.S. Department of the Treasury.

Chart 3.2. Disposition of TARP Bank Funds.

IV. Stress Tests

Five Years Ago

- **Despite the initial round of TARP bank investments in fall of 2008, markets remained leery of the potential for significant bank failures** as continued write-downs and losses at banks unnerved investors and counterparties and exacerbated the severe funding pressures institutions faced in the capital markets.
- **After billions of dollars in losses, core capital ratios at many of the largest U.S. banks fell to levels at which investors and counterparties had little confidence that they could withstand** the tough economic environment and ongoing market challenges.
- **This lack of certainty and transparency about the financial health of these banks made it extremely difficult for them to raise capital from private sources.** Accordingly, policymakers worried that – even if these banks survived – they would hoard capital and withhold lending as an alternative to raising capital. In particular, many observers were concerned that this cycle would be exacerbated if the economy weakened further and home prices continued falling.

Obama Administration Actions

The Administration Took Immediate Action to Stabilize and Strengthen the Financial System through Comprehensive Stress Tests

- **In February 2009, the Administration and regulators announced comprehensive stress tests of the nation's largest banks to reduce uncertainty regarding their solvency and to help stabilize the financial system.** Treasury indicated any bank found to have an insufficient amount of capital to continue normal operations would be forced to raise capital, preferably from private sources but, if necessary, through a government backstop program that was established.
- **The stress tests, designed and administered by the Federal Reserve and other bank regulators, were intended to reassure markets that banks would have the capital to continue lending even if economic conditions continued to deteriorate,** as it tested bank finances against an adverse economic scenario to help ensure

that banks would remain solvent and in a position to continue extending credit to the real economy even under severe conditions. This rigorous stress testing concluded under the more adverse scenario that losses at the largest banks could be $600 billion, or 9.1 percent of loan balances – a two-year loss rate higher than during the historical peak loss years of the 1930s.

- **The results of the stress tests were viewed as credible, restoring investor confidence.** The results indicated that 10 of the 19 stress tested banks would need to raise a total of $75 billion in capital under the more adverse scenario in order to be appropriately capitalized and serve their customers.

Five Years Later

- **The stress tests worked**. Shortly after the release of the results, the largest banks in the country raised over $80 billion of equity capital from private sources, with no major banks requiring additional government support outside of an investment through the auto program in GMAC.
- **The increased capital and certainty resulting from the stress tests proved a turning point in the crisis,** encouraging many market participants, investors, and businesses to conclude the worst was behind us and that the banking system would remain solvent and functioning. This in turn increased market participants' comfort with making investments in the financial markets and the broader US economy.
- **Today, stress tests modeled after the crisis-era stress tests have been adopted as part of the regular supervisory framework in the United States and help ensure banks have enough capital to weather future downturns.** Dodd-Frank requires stress tests that quantitatively assess how bank capital levels would fare in stressful economic and financial scenarios, and the Federal Reserve combines the quantitative results from those stress tests with more qualitative assessments of the capital planning processes used by banks.
- **Stress tests have been increasingly adopted as a norm in the global regulatory community** as central banks and banking regulators throughout the world have recognized their value in helping ensure a safe banking system and in maintaining market confidence.

V. American International Group (AIG)

Five Years Ago

AIG – The World's Largest Insurer – Was on the Brink of Collapse

- **AIG's derivatives trading led to substantial losses, placing the entire company at risk.** As a result of AIG's significant involvement in credit default swaps (CDSs) – a contract that provides protection against losses on bonds – the company lost nearly $18 billion in the first 9 months of 2008. As expectations of borrower defaults rose and its credit ratings fell, AIG had to post additional cash collateral against potential losses on its CDS trades and other insurance policies, which further weakened the company.
- **As the financial crisis worsened and the markets froze, AIG was unable to borrow to meet its cash needs, bringing it to the brink of collapse**. Mounting losses in its CDS and securities lending businesses and growing demand for cash collateral against future losses created a dire need for additional capital at AIG. With the credit markets frozen amid the worst financial crisis since the Great Depression, AIG had no sources of funding to meet its obligations and was faced with certain bankruptcy.
- **Regulatory gaps in derivatives complicated the response to the AIG crisis**. The widespread use of derivatives, such as CDS, had allowed many firms to build up substantial off-balance sheet leverage and hidden risks. These derivatives were largely unregulated, which not only led to direct losses, but created uncertainty among counterparties, investors, and regulators concerning exposures to AIG.
- **As the world's largest insurer, AIG was too interconnected with other major financial firms and the consequences of its failure during a period of acute financial stress would have sent a tremendous shock through the global economy**. The collapse of AIG at that time would have triggered billions of dollars in losses at other financial firms that purchased CDS protection and insurance from AIG, potentially sending many of these firms into failure as well. Lacking the tools for an orderly resolution, policy makers feared that using bankruptcy to resolve a company of AIG's scale could lead

to additional market disruptions that would have further undermined the safety and soundness of the financial system.

- **Observers predicted any federal bailout of AIG would have resulted in substantial losses to the American taxpayers from $36-$45 billion.** CBO at one point estimated that the AIG bailout would cost taxpayers $36 billion, while other estimates showed losses north of $45 billion.
- **Lacking any viable alternatives, the federal government stepped in to commit more than $182 billion to stabilize AIG during the financial crisis.** Without existing tools to resolve a large, complex financial firm like AIG, the Federal Reserve provided up to $85 billion of funding support through a credit facility to prevent the collapse of AIG in the fall of 2008, and an additional $37.8 billion was committed to AIG less than a month later. In addition, Treasury committed $70 billion in two TARP investment transactions in AIG.

Obama Administration Actions

- **The Administration took immediate steps to restructure AIG and accelerate the timeline for AIG's repayment of the government's support.** Under its restructuring plan, Treasury and the Federal Reserve Bank of New York (FRBNY) worked with AIG to fundamentally restructure AIG's balance sheet and its business operations, winding down riskier parts of the business, and selling non-core assets.
- **The Administration pursued reforms to ensure that this type of bailout never occurs again.** As part of Wall Street Reform, the Administration sought to put in place a comprehensive regulatory framework for derivatives, ensure policy makers and regulators have an effective resolution regime for winding down failed financial institutions, reduce the complexity and interconnectedness of the largest institutions, and give regulators the authority to better regulate institutions whose failure would threaten the system.

Five Years Later

The Obama Administration Turned a Profit on Its Support for AIG, and Is Taking Steps to Ensure That This Type of Bailout Never Occurs Again

- **Rather than lose tens of billions of dollars, the Administration successfully recouped the federal government's full support for AIG, along with positive returns of nearly $23 billion.** Despite widespread predictions that the American taxpayers stood to lose billions on its $182.3 billion of assistance to AIG, the Administration successfully recouped more than $205 billion, for a total positive return to the taxpayers of $22.7 billion, while AIG's loan to the Federal Reserve was fully repaid.
- **Key Wall Street reforms have been passed into law and are being implemented to prevent the problems that arose with AIG from happening again, including the FSOC designation of AIG for enhanced standards and oversight by the Federal Reserve.** The Financial Stability Oversight Council (FSOC) designation of AIG will subject it to enhanced prudential standards and Federal Reserve regulation including tough capital, liquidity, and stress testing requirements. In addition, the Securities and Exchange Commission (SEC) and Commodity Futures Trading Commission (CFTC) have made substantial progress in implementing new OTC derivative reform requirements like central clearing of standardized OTC derivatives as well as better reporting and transparency. The U.S. has led international bank and securities regulators to agree to adopt similar rules globally. The FDIC has also made substantial progress in implementing its new resolution regime that will ensure that firms like AIG can be resolved without posing a threat to financial stability.

VI. Automotive Industry

Five Years Ago

When President Obama Took Office, the American Automobile Industry Was in Crisis

- **In late 2008, the combination of a historic recession and financial crisis combined with earlier struggles pushed the American auto industry to the brink of collapse.** Access to credit for car loans dried up and auto sales plunged 40 percent. As a result, auto manufacturers and suppliers dramatically curtailed production and shed jobs.

- **The Bush Administration extended short-term loans to GM and Chrysler to keep the companies afloat.** Amid the worst financial crisis since the Great Depression, credit markets were frozen and alternative sources of financing dried up, forcing GM and Chrysler to either seek government support or face near certain liquidations. In response, the Bush Administration extended short-term bridge loans to GM and Chrysler but left open key decisions on how to address the crisis, in part to preserve flexibility for the incoming Administration.
- **There was significant public opposition to government intervention.** Many public commentators urged inaction, arguing that the federal government should let the auto companies fail. Some observers warned that government intervention would hurt the overall economy and result in even higher unemployment.
- **The collapse of GM and Chrysler would have had a cascading effect through the American economy.** Similar to other parts of our economy, the American automotive industry has grown increasingly interconnected. The survival of the American auto manufacturers was critical to the health of its suppliers, auto dealers, and the thousands of small businesses in communities with high concentrations of auto workers. And because Ford and other auto companies depended on those same suppliers, the collapse of GM and Chrysler could have caused the failure of other auto companies as well. In fact, observers estimated that the bankruptcy of GM and Chrysler could have resulted in1 million jobs lost.
- **The failure of GM and Chrysler would have also resulted in significant government liabilities.** Had GM and Chrysler failed, the government and the American taxpayers would have borne substantial costs in providing social safety support and healthcare to workers and communities devastated by the crisis.

Obama Administration Actions

To Avoid the Collapse of the Auto Industry, the Administration Intervened to Stabilize GM and Chrysler and Protect American Manufacturing Jobs

- **Against the vocal opposition from public commentators, the President decided to stand behind the American auto industry**

and protect manufacturing jobs through additional financial support. The Administration rejected initial restructuring plans from GM and Chrysler, challenging them to develop more aggressive blueprints to return to viability. In response, both GM and Chrysler developed substantially more forward-leaning plans to restore financial viability even in a challenging economic environment.

- **Launched "Cash for Clunkers" to support demand for the auto industry:** In July 2009, the Administration launched "Cash for Clunkers," which provided $3,500 or $4,500 rebates to auto buyers. The program provided critical support to the auto industry at the height of the crisis, sparking nearly 700,000 in auto sales that some analysts estimate generated more than $25 billion in economic activity.

Five Years Later

As a Result of Actions Taken to Stabilize the Auto Industry, Auto Manufacturers Are Once Again Profitable, Competitive, and Growing

- **The big three American automakers are profitable.** In 2011, the auto industry reached an important milestone when all three major American automakers posted net profits for the first time since 2004. In fact, each of the Big Three have posted positive net income every year since. The growing profitability of the American auto industry is reflected in the growing value of GM and Ford, which are both up more than 50% over the past year.
- **The American auto sales are growing – with GM sales at their highest level since 2008 and Chrysler reporting 41 straight months of improving sales.** Supported by the orderly restructuring enabled by federal assistance, the American auto industry is growing again. In August 2013, GM posted its best month of sales since 2008 and Ford its best month since 2006, while Chrysler reported its 41st straight month of year-over-year sales gains. In fact, overall American auto sales in August 2013 were higher and grew faster than any month since 2007.
- **The Big Three automakers all gained market share for the first time in 23 years.** After years of steady market share declines, in 2011, Ford, GM, and Chrysler gained market shares in the United States for the first time since 1988. This represented an incredible

resurgence of the American auto industry, just two years after the near collapse of GM and Chrysler.

- **Exports of American autos are higher now than ever.** In 2012, more than 1 million cars and trucks were exported from US factories, the highest recorded in history and more than a threefold increase from 2003.
- **The number of American auto manufacturing jobs is growing again**. Since June 2009, the American auto industry has created more than 340,000 jobs. In fact, since 2009, 1 in every 4 manufacturing jobs added in the U.S. came from the auto industry. The non-partisan Center for Automotive Research estimated that 1.45 million Americans are working as a direct result of the auto bailout both at the automakers and associated businesses downstream in the economy.
- **American taxpayers are being paid back significantly more than expected.** Despite the chorus of warnings that the government would not recoup the vast majority of its investments in the auto companies, American taxpayers are seeing progress. Chrysler repaid its loans to the government 6 years ahead of schedule, returning 90% of the total invested. The Treasury has also recovered a substantial portion of its investments in GM and plans to fully exit the company in the coming year. Ally, formerly known as GMAC, also recently announced a plan to pay the government back another $6 billion; Treasury is continuing to work with the company to recover its remaining investment.

VII. HOUSING

Five Years Ago

- **Home prices had fallen by 19% since a year earlier**, the largest one year drop in home prices ever measured, and leaving over 10 million borrowers underwater. Some cities were hit even worse, with areas like Phoenix and Las Vegas seeing declines of greater than 50 percent.
- **Housing starts had plummeted nearly 80 percent from their peak** to a level below 500,000.
- **Both new and existing home sales were near all-time lows** under 500,000 and 4 million respectively.

- **Millions of homeowners faced distress**, with around three million seriously delinquent borrowers.
- **More than 100,000 construction jobs were being lost each month**, with the fall in residential construction reducing GDP by 1 percent in the prior year.

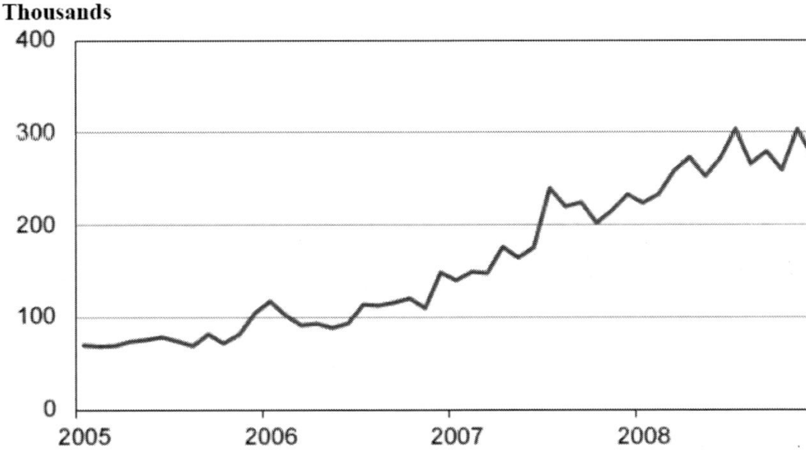

Source: RealtyTrac, Inc., Bloomberg.

Chart 7.1. U.S. Foreclosure Filings per Month.

Obama Administration Actions

The Administration Took Immediate Action to Stabilize and Heal Our Housing Market

- **Home Affordable Modification Program (HAMP) was launched to help borrowers avoid foreclosure** by making their payments more affordable through permanent loan modifications.
- **The Administration worked with regulators to help responsible underwater borrowers refinance through the Home Affordable Refinancing Program (HARP) and FHA's Streamline and Short Refinance Programs.**
- **As private lenders exited the mortgage market, the Federal Housing Administration (FHA) stepped up its lending,** playing a critical counter-cyclical role that helped ensure the continued flow of mortgage credit to consumers all while taking steps to strengthen the

program and rebuild its reserves for the long term. According to independent analysis, absent FHA interventions, mortgage interest rates would have doubled and home prices would have fallen by an additional 25 percent.

- **The Hardest Hit Fund (HHF) committed $7.6 billion in resources to states to develop locally-tailored programs that assist struggling homeowners.**
- **A number of programs targeted the uneven recovery to help communities stabilize.** The Neighborhood Stabilization Program (NSP) allocated $7 billion to thousands of neighborhoods to address foreclosed and abandoned homes, HUD's Homeless Prevention and Rapid Rehousing Program helped Americans that were homeless or at risk of becoming homeless due to the financial crisis get promptly rehoused or access assistance to remain housed, and HUD's Tax Credit Assistance Program and Treasury's Credit Exchange Program protected the affordable rental housing market, ensuring development continued when markets froze.
- **HUD launched an Office of Housing Counseling** and worked with HUD-approved housing counselors to assist over 9 million families in making smart and informed financial decisions.
- **The Administration created the Consumer Financial Protection Bureau** (CFPB) to better protect borrowers and make buying a home a simpler and safer process.
- **Expanded refinancing for underwater borrowers through** additional flexibilities in Home Affordable Refinancing Program 2.0 (HARP) and FHA Streamline Refinance Program.
- **The Administration tripled incentives for principal reduction in HAMP to help underwater homeowners.**
- **The National Mortgage Servicing Settlement was negotiated along with 49 state Attorneys General** to hold banks accountable and assist struggling homeowners. Over 1.5 million homeowners have received more than $50 billion in committed relief due to the National Mortgage Servicing Settlement.
- **DOJ has brought 1,600 mortgage fraud cases against 3,000 defendants** over last three years, and has collected more money for victims of housing discrimination in the last fiscal year than in the previous 23 years combined.

- **Through HAMP and FHA, unemployed borrowers can delay payments on their mortgages for up to 12 months** while they are looking for a job, up from a 3 month limitation.
- **The Administration continued to help state and local housing finance agencies through the New Issue Bond Program to extend affordable mortgage credit** to more than 135,000 working families and enable the development and rehabilitation of 40,000 affordable rental units.
- **The Administration partnered with 3,000 American Jobs Centers to provide housing counseling to help unemployed homeowners avoid foreclosure.**
- **The HUD Distressed Asset Stabilization Program was launched to require investors who purchase FHA non-performing loans in hardest hit areas to commit to managing the property in a manner that avoids foreclosure, vacancy and abandonment.**
- **The FHA "Back to Work Initiative" was established to create a path to homeownership for** borrowers whose credit suffered during the crisis because of circumstances beyond their control.

Five Years Later

- **HAMP led to 7 million homeowners getting government or private mortgage modifications – twice as many as those who went through foreclosure during the Obama Presidency.** The program has directly helped more than 1.2 million borrowers to date and an additional 1.9 million homeowners have received foreclosure prevention assistance through the Federal Housing Administration (FHA). The Administration's programs continue to encourage improved standards and processes in the industry, with private sector lenders offering families and individuals more than 3.7 million proprietary mortgage modifications. Collectively, nearly 7 million homeowners have received some form of relief since April 2009.
- **Tripled incentives for principal reduction in HAMP to help underwater homeowners.** In recent months, approximately 70 percent of eligible borrowers in HAMP have received some form of principal reduction. Prior to the introduction of principal reduction in HAMP, only about 1 percent of all loan modifications included principal reduction.

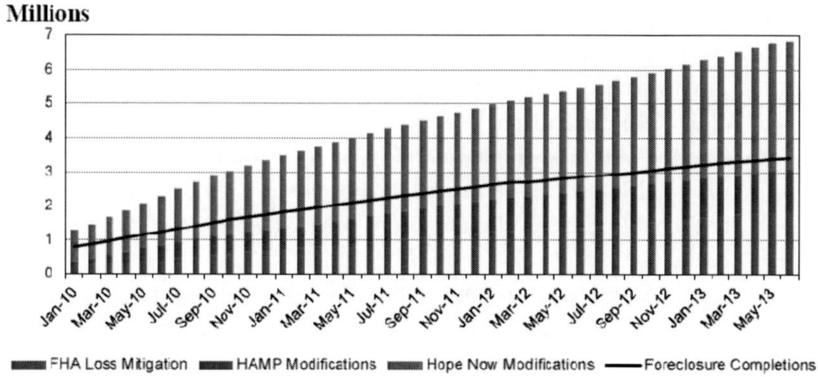

Source: Source: U.S. Department of Housing and Urban Development, U.S. Department of the Treasury, Hope Now Alliance, and RealtyTrac.

Chart 7.2. Cumulative Mortgages Receiving Aid and Mortgages Foreclosed.

- **Worked with states to use HHF for blight elimination.** Michigan plans to use $100 million of its existing HHF allocation for demolition and greening of blighted properties, and Ohio plans to use $60 million to support blight elimination in their communities.
- **Refinancing nearly tripled after the introduction of HARP 2.0, from 400,000 in 2011 to 1.1 million in 2012**, bringing the total number of families that have refinanced under HARP to more than 2.8 million through July 2013 and saving the average family $3,000 a year.
- **Home building is coming back, leading to an upswing in construction jobs.** Recent housing starts are up roughly 75 percent from their April 2009 bottom of 478,000, while the number of residential construction jobs is on the rebound.
- **Existing home sales have increased 47.2 percent** from their crisis low and are approaching historical norms of about 5.0 million units.
- **Housing wealth is growing again, with owners' equity up $2.8 trillion** since hitting a low at the beginning of 2009. This in turn has contributed to increased economic activity through consumer spending, small business investment, and more.
- **Home prices are rising at the fastest pace in seven years**, up more than 12 percent in the past year. Rising prices have brought nearly 5 million families out from being underwater in the last 6 quarters.

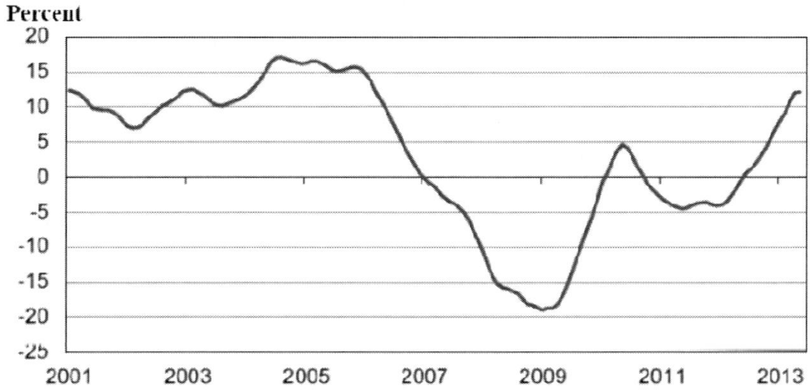

Source: Bloomberg.

Chart 7.3. Case-Shiller 20 City Home Prices YoY % Δ.

- **Still, more work remains to be done to improve wider access to affordable mortgage credit,** address the uneven recovery across communities, and move to a more sustainable equilibrium where government does not back such a high percentage of the mortgage market.
- **Going forward, we also need to end the failed business model of Fannie Mae and Freddie Mac,** putting private capital at the center of the housing finance system while preserving access to a 30 year fixed rate mortgage for creditworthy borrowers.

VIII. Small Business

Five Years Ago

With Banks on the Edge of Collapse and Weak Consumer Demand, Small Businesses, the Traditional Engine of Our Economy, Struggled under the Weight of the Great Recession

- **Reduction in credit availability had a disproportionate impact on small businesses.** Collapse in bank lending dramatically reduced credit availability for small businesses, even when loans were Small Business Administration (SBA) guaranteed. From their peak in 2007 through 2010, the number of small business loans declined by 68 percent.

- **Declining home and asset value dramatically reduced availability of collateral.** With falling commercial and residential real estate values, traditional sources of small business collateral disappeared. This further reduced small businesses' ability to obtain needed capital.
- **Small businesses experienced a spike in bankruptcies.** In 2006, fewer than 20,000 US companies filed for bankruptcy protection while in 2009 the number of firms declaring bankruptcy jumped to 61,000. Many of these firms were small businesses. In fact, small businesses lost 40 percent more jobs than larger firms during the Great Recession.
- **American economy lost a critical driver of growth.** Over the last two decades, small and new businesses have been responsible for creating two out of every three net new jobs. The decline in small business creation and growth undermined an important engine of growth for the American economy.

Obama Administration Actions

The Administration Took Immediate Actions to Invest in Entrepreneurship and Small Businesses

- **Supported small businesses through TARP programs.** Treasury established the Community Development Capital Initiative (CDCI) and administered the Capital Purchase Program (CPP) to stabilize small and large banks across the country. Over 90 percent of CPP and CDCI participants were banks with less than $10 billion in assets, nearly 70 percent were small banks with assets under $1 billion, and the median size of CPP banks was approximately $500 million in assets.
- **Treasury supported the liquidity of key SBA lending program.** At the depth of the Great Recession, even government guaranteed small business lending was frozen. To ensure that small business continued to access needed capital, Treasury stepped in to support liquidity by purchasing the government guaranteed portion of SBA 7(a) loans. Treasury also increased the level of guarantees it provided in SBA 7(a) and decreased the fees paid by small businesses. By January 2012, when Treasury closed the program, $367 million of small business loans were supported through the program and taxpayers earned a return of $9 million.

- **The President championed key legislation to cut taxes and support small businesses.** The President championed and signed key legislation to support the growth of small businesses, including the American Recovery and Reinvestment Act of 2009 as well as the most significant small business legislation in over a decade (Small Business Jobs Act of 2010) and legislation to make it easier for small businesses to raise capital (Jumpstart Our Business Startups Act of 2012). These bills supported the record expansion of SBA's lending programs, and created critical new programs, including the Small Business Lending Fund (SBLF) to support bank lending to small business and the State Small Business Credit Initiative (SSBCI) to bolster state and local programs that help small businesses access credit.
- **Increased the number of lenders that participate in SBA programs.** SBA lending programs today include more than 1,000 additional community banks, and many more mission-based lenders that are supporting more small businesses and entrepreneurs across the country, oftentimes in the communities hit hardest by the financial crisis.

Five Years Later

Today Small Businesses Are Making a Remarkable Comeback, and Are Once Again the Engine of Job and Economic Growth

- **SBLF successfully increased the amount of capital available for small business.** As of March 31, 2013, SBLF participants increased their small business lending by $9.0 billion over a $36.3 billion pre-program baseline. Over 80 percent of these participants had increased their lending by 10 percent or more.
- **SSBCI successfully leveraged state and local resources to support lending to small businesses.** As of September 2013, Treasury disbursed over $870 million in SSBCI funds, which supported $1.9 billion in private loans and investments in small businesses as of the end of 2012. These funds have helped support thousands of small businesses, with nearly 80 percent of SSBCI loans or investments going to businesses with fewer than 10 employees.
- **President championed critical tax relief to small business owners.** The President championed and signed a total of 18 tax cuts for small

businesses. These tax cuts have helped more small businesses invest in expanding their businesses and create new jobs.

- **The cost of borrowing for small business is coming down**. Cost of borrowing for small business relative to larger businesses has declined for 10 straight quarters.
- **More small businesses are getting approved for loans**. Approvals for small business lending have been making a comeback. In November 2012, small banks approved more small business loans than they rejected for the first time since the recession. Over the last 4 years, SBA supported more than $106 billion in lending to more than 193,000 small businesses and entrepreneurs. This includes two record years of delivering over $30 billion in loan guarantees annually.
- **Terms of small business loans are easing**. Loan officers reported easing of credit terms in nine of the past 10 quarters. And demand for loans from small businesses either increased or stayed flat in seven of the past eight quarters, with the highest recorded demand since 2005 coming in the first half of 2012.
- **Administration put focus on small business contracting**. In the last three years, small businesses accessed more than $286.3 billion dollars in federal contracts. That is $32 billion more than the previous three years, despite an overall decline in spending during those years.
- **1 million small businesses and entrepreneurs are receiving training each year.** SBA's national network of district offices, Small Business Development Centers, and Women's Business Centers help train 1 million small business owners and entrepreneurs every single year.

IX. Consumer Lending

Five Years Ago

- **The collapse of Lehman Brothers in September 2008 led to widespread panic and a "run" on many of the key sources of funding for financial institutions.** Losses on Lehman debt led to withdrawals from money market mutual funds (MMFs) and a contraction in the commercial paper market used by corporations to finance their businesses.

- **As capital markets froze and funding dried up, banks reduced lending to consumers and businesses to conserve liquidity.** The nation's largest banks reduced loans to consumers by 79 percent in 2008, and consumer credit became virtually inaccessible. Nearly $2 trillion in lending capacity – half of all money loaned to business and consumers in 2007 – disappeared. Americans were unable to finance necessities like mortgages, automobiles, education, or credit cards.
- **Increasing job loss and decline in income as a result of the Great Recession made it more difficult for millions of Americans to meet their debt obligations**. By 2009, the delinquency rate and severe delinquency rates on consumer loans had roughly tripled and quadrupled, respectively, in just 3 years.

Obama Administration Actions

The Administration Took Immediate Action to Increase the Flow of Credit and to Provide Help to Struggling Americans

- **The Administration took steps to restart frozen credit markets.** The expanded Term Asset-Backed Securities Loan Facility (TALF), jointly announced with the Federal Reserve, helped revitalize securitization markets by encouraging investors to buy securities backed by consumer loans. Independent analysis has found that TALF played a crucial role in restoring liquidity and thus preventing the shutdown of consumer credit markets during the brunt of the crisis. Aiding TALF was the new Public-Private Investment Program (PPIP), which successfully supported the markets for legacy mortgage-backed securities and contributed to ensuring credit markets remained open for households and businesses.
- **The Helping Families Save their Homes Act of 2009 reinvigorated the flow of credit in the economy** by extending temporary increases in deposit insurance and increasing the borrowing authority of the Federal Deposit Insurance Corporation (FDIC). The act also ensured credit unions could continue to make credit available by increasing the borrowing authority of the National Credit Union Administration (NCUA).
- **As private lenders exited the mortgage market, the Federal Housing Administration (FHA) stepped up its lending, playing a critical counter-cyclical role that helped ensure the continued flow**

of mortgage credit to consumers. According to independent analysis, absent FHA interventions, mortgage interest rates would have doubled and home prices would have fallen by an additional 25 percent.

- **TARP's Auto Industry Financing Program (AIFP) stepped in to support the financing arms of the auto industry.** The support of General Motors Acceptance Corporation (GMAC) and other auto financing firms ensured that consumers had access to financing when making auto purchases and further bolstered the auto industry during a critical time. This program also provided support for dealers and enabled them to be able to keep cars on their lots.

Five Years Later

- **The Administration's response unclogged the credit pipes of the financial system, improving credit access for borrowers while lowering borrowing costs.** Since the recession, the prices of auto loans and credit card borrowing have improved substantially.

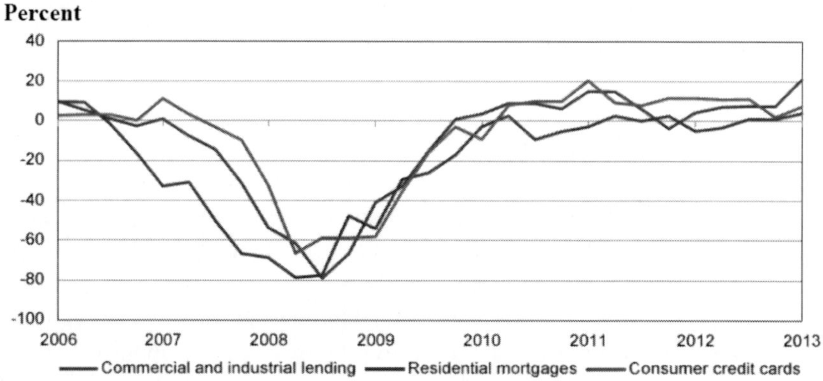

Source: Federal Reserve Senior Loan Officer Opinion Survey.

Chart 9.1. Net Percentage of Banks Easing Lending.

- **Banks have begun easing their lending standards and have reported stronger consumer demand in most loan categories.**
- **Since 2009, the percentage of delinquent household debts has significantly decreased, from 11.9 percent to 8.6 perecnt.** However,

more work remains to be done, as this remains significantly above pre-crisis levels and the share of seriously delinquent debts remains stubbornly high.

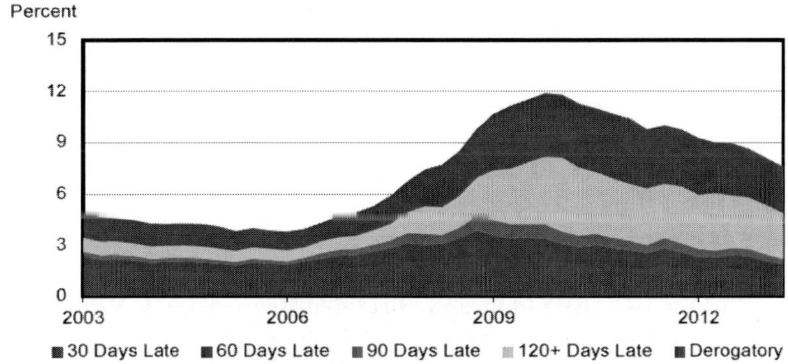

Source: FRBNY Consumer Credit Panel, Equifax, Haver Analytics.

Note: Derogatory loans are loans for which there are reports of a repossession, charge off to bad debt, or foreclosure.

Chart 9.2. Share of Household Debt by Delinquency Status.

- **Low interest rates, less borrowing, and increases in employment and income have reduced the household debt service ratio to a historic low,** reducing households' debt repayments and freeing up income for other spending.

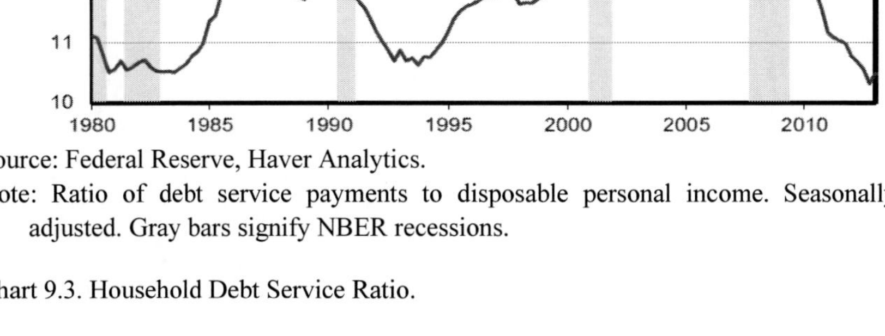

Source: Federal Reserve, Haver Analytics.

Note: Ratio of debt service payments to disposable personal income. Seasonally adjusted. Gray bars signify NBER recessions.

Chart 9.3. Household Debt Service Ratio.

- **Non-mortgage consumer credit growth has picked up, with auto loans and student loans accounting for most of this increase.** In the former case, the widespread availability of credit and rising consumer demand for motor vehicles has led to the strong recovery of auto loans. However, the high rate of student loan delinquencies means that more work is required to stop growing student debt burdens.

X. HOUSEHOLD WEALTH

Five Years Ago

- **In the two years before the President took office, U.S. households lost a staggering $17 trillion dollars in wealth.** The median family's net wealth dropped by $11,400 in this two year period, a loss of 18.1 percent. This loss was broad-based, with over 60 percent of American families seeing their wealth decline between 2007 and 2009 as the recession took its toll.
- **Americans lost $5.6 trillion in home equity during the same period.** Across the nation, home prices plummeted, dropping approximately one-third from their peak in 2006 to the beginning of 2009.

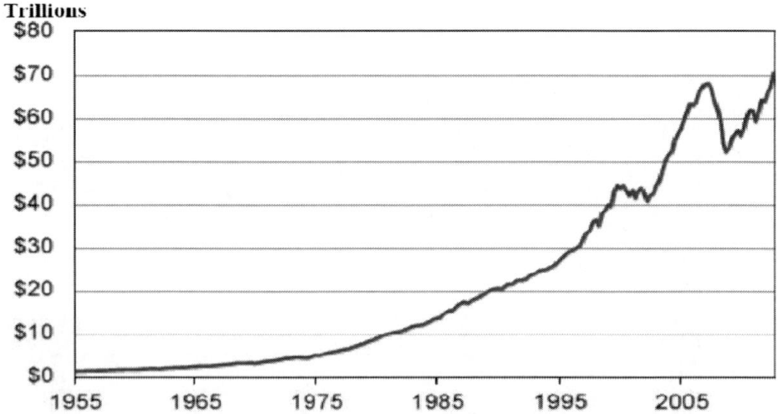

Source: Federal Reserve, Bloomberg.
Chart 10.1. Household Net Worth.

- **Assets in retirement accounts such as 401(k)s dropped $2.8 trillion** between September 2007 and December 2008. Equity indices worldwide fell by more than 40 percent in 2008, with the S&P 500 dropping by 688 points from 1,496 in 2007 to 808 in early 2009 – the largest single-year decline in decades.
- **While the majority of American families were hit by the recession, vulnerable groups were especially devastated.** Young people, those with less education, and members of historically disadvantaged minority groups were particularly hard-hit.

Obama Administration Actions

The Administration Took Immediate Actions to Help Struggling Families

- **Signed into law the $800 billion Recovery Act within 30 days of taking office.** With leadership and support from the President, Congress passed the American Recovery and Reinvestment Act, which was signed into law by President Obama on February 17. The Act was necessary to stem the tide as demand in the U.S. and around the world continued to contract.
- **In addition to Administration efforts to stabilize the financial system and the economy, the President prioritized further help for middle class and working families by signing into law tax relief legislation.**
    - **The President signed into law the American Opportunity Tax Credit**, worth $10,000 over four years and currently helping 9 million families cover the cost of college.
    - **By increasing the Earned Income Tax Credit,** the Administration helped moderate-income working families make ends meet. The Recovery Act increased the credit for families with three or more children, bringing the maximum amount to $5,657.
    - **The Child Tax Credit was expanded,** helping low-and moderate-income families with children, by reducing the minimum amount of earned income used to calculate the additional child tax credit to $3,000 from $12,550.
    - **The Administration negotiated a bipartisan agreement that led to a payroll tax cut for 160 million working Americans,**

giving them in effect a 2 percent raise through the end of 2012. A family earning $50,000 got a tax cut of $1,000.

- **The Administration took unprecedented actions to stabilize housing markets and prevent further loss in home equity.** The government's foreclosure prevention efforts kept millions of families in their homes through programs such as the Home Affordable Modification Program (HAMP), the Hardest Hit Fund (HHF), and the Home Affordable Refinancing Program (HARP).
- **The Affordable Care Act gave families additional security during difficult financial times.** Nearly 17 million children can no longer be denied care due to a pre-existing condition, 6.6 million young adults can stay on their parent's insurance through age 26, and more than 5 million seniors have saved an average of $768 each on the cost of their prescription drugs. The Act also ends lifetime caps on how much care insurers will pay for and requires insurance companies to spend at least 80 cents of a premium dollar on health care or improvements to care.

Five Years Later

- **By the end of 2012, Americans had recovered $14.7 trillion of aggregate household net worth, recouping 91 percent of the recession losses.**
- **Housing wealth is up $2.8 trillion since hitting a low at the beginning of 2009.** This in turn has contributed to increased economic activity through consumer spending, small business investment, and more. Home prices are rising at the fastest pace in seven years, up more than 12 percent in the past year. Rising prices brought 5 million families out from being underwater in the last 6 quarters.
- **Retirement assets and other financial assets have made significant gains since 2009.** Stock markets continue to rally, with the S&P 500 up over 100 percent during President Obama's Administration.
- **Strong employment growth has also aided in household wealth recovery; as of July 2013, the economy had added private sector jobs for 42 consecutive months,** and a total of 7.5 million jobs have been added over that period. American manufacturers have added

more than 500,000 jobs since January 2010, the strongest period of job growth since 1989.

- **While much has been accomplished, there is still work left to do.** While the majority of wealth lost during the recession has been recovered, that recovery has not been felt equally across the socioeconomic spectrum. Adjusted for inflation and population growth, only 45 percent of wealth lost during the recession has been recovered, and many of the hardest hit households did not benefit as much from the rebound in financial assets prices.

XI. CONSUMER PROTECTIONS & CFPB

Five Years Ago

The Financial Crisis Demonstrated One of the Most Glaring Gaps in Our Regulatory Framework – The Absence of a Watchdog Agency to Protect Consumers for Financial Products and Services

- **In the lead-up to the foreclosure crisis, some lenders engaged in predatory lending practices that misled families to take on mortgages for homes they could not afford.** These practices included offering "no doc" and "low doc" mortgages, where a borrower's financial situation and ability to repay a loan was not appropriately taken into account. Some banks also offered "interest only" mortgages that resulted in unpredictable and fluctuating monthly payments. And in other instances, hidden fees and misleading marketing tactics were used against the interest of the borrower.
- **Regulation of certain consumer financial industries, including payday lenders, consumer reporting agencies and debt collection agencies was inadequate.** Many financial activities fell outside of a rigorous regulatory framework. As a result, some consumer financial industries, including payday lending and debt collection, operated without adequate safeguards for consumers.
- **Federal agencies and state agencies lacked a regulatory system of cooperation to enforce consumer financial protection laws.** The lack of collaboration resulted in counterproductive regulatory actions undermining the impact of consumer financial protection laws.

- **No single federal agency existed whose primary mission was to protect consumers from irresponsible financial practices.**

Obama Administration Actions

- **The President fought for and signed into law the strongest consumer financial protections in history with the Dodd-Frank Wall Street Reform and Consumer Protection Act.** The Dodd-Frank Act consolidated the consumer protection authorities of seven regulators into one agency, the Consumer Financial Protection Bureau (CFPB) and tasked it with a single job: to protect families when they make important financial decisions.
- **The Administration acted aggressively to hold financial firms accountable for their actions,** including:
  - The largest mortgage settlement in history that have helped 1.5 million homeowners receive more than $50 billion in relief
  - More money for victims of housing discrimination in the last fiscal year than in the previous 23 years combined
  - More than 1,600 mortgage and financial fraud cases brought by DOJ against 3,000 defendants over last three years

Five Years Later

The CFPB Established Safer Lending Standards, Is Working to Make Financial Education, Assistance, and Disclosures More Accessible, and Provides Federal Supervision and Accountability

- **The CFPB established safer national mortgage standards to protect middle class families.** The CFPB created safe mortgage standards for loans that meet Ability-to-Repay requirements by requiring lenders to determine that a borrower can repay both the principal and interest of a mortgage loan over the long term, based upon the borrower's income, debt, and other factors.
- **The Bureau has launched new requirements and initiatives to help ensure that the mortgage and other consumer lending processes are transparent and straightforward, and empowered consumers with the financial information necessary for borrowing decisions. Efforts by the CFPB include:**

    - New requirements to provide consumers with clear monthly mortgage statements, warnings before interest rates adjust for adjustable rate mortgages and the right to dispute errors.
    - A "Know Before You Owe" campaign so consumers and lenders are able to view the costs and risks before closing on a mortgage.
    - A requirement that borrowers receive housing counseling before a high-cost mortgage is made.
    - A single, simple mortgage disclosure form to guarantee that integrated mortgage disclosures are transparent and improve consumers' understanding of their mortgage loans.
    - A complaint hotline, which has handled 175,000 complaints from consumers in every state around the country.
    - Assistance for consumers by working with their financial institution to solve specific problems.
    - Caps on fees and points that can be charged by lenders for mortgages.
    - Qualification standards on lenders including criminal record checks and training requirements.
- **Federal supervision of lenders became an institutional component of federal lending regulation to foster compliance with newly imposed restrictions, standards, and federal consumer financial laws.** Consumer reporting agencies, debt collection agencies, and payday lenders are subjected to federal supervision for the first time, affecting over 200 million consumers. Additionally, all banks with $10 billion or more in assets and all nonbank financial institutions that participate in the mortgage market are all federally supervised.
- **The President improved governmental cooperation in enforcing consumer financial protection laws,** by leading the Department of Justice to execute agreements with various federal and state agencies to address overlapping authorities and regulatory powers.
- **The CFPB took enforcement actions resulting in companies refunding over $400 million to over 6 million consumers** so that money is returned to consumers for deceptive marketing and unreasonable fees. The CFPB has brought enforcement actions and obtained consent orders from the banks for unfair, deceptive, and abusive card practices. The Department of Justice has brought over 1,600 mortgage fraud cases against almost 3,000 defendants.

XII. PREVENTING EXCESSIVE RISK TAKING

Five Years Ago

- **The increasing use of securitization to fund loans without appropriate safeguards led to a decline in underwriting standards.** Originators made loans that were then packaged by securitizers, who in turn sold them as securities to investors. Because these securities could be readily sold, originators and securitizers had little interest in whether the borrowers would be able to repay their loans. Without a financial incentive to perform due diligence or verify underwriting quality, underwriting standards for new loans fell and excessively risky asset-backed securities flooded the market.
- **Other, large-scale bank-like activities outside of the regulated banking system grew significantly prior to the crisis**. In the lead up to the financial crisis, firms that were not subject to banking regulations became large sources of mortgage, consumer, and corporate credit. These entities included asset back commercial paper conduits, structured investment vehicles (SIVs), and some hedge funds. These "shadow-banking" entities often made money by borrowing short and lending on a longer-term, higher-yield basis, much like banks. But unlike banks, such activities were funded by the short-term debt markets, not deposits, and lacked the supervisory and regulatory standards of the traditional banking system. When the recession hit, these entities were forced to liquidate as the markets were no longer willing to lend to them. This resulted in a rapid contraction in credit and often "fire sales" of assets at depressed prices.
- **Many of the largest banks took on excessive risks, relied on less stable forms of funding, and lacked sufficient capital and liquidity.** As losses mounted in housing related assets, particularly in subprime asset backed securities and off-balance sheet vehicles in 2007 and 2008, market participants feared that bank capital levels would prove inadequate to absorb ongoing losses. This was exacerbated by speculative positions banks took prior to the financial crisis that suffered losses and sponsored investment vehicles that were sold to their clients and required extraordinary support.
- **In addition to engaging in risky, non-traditional banking activities, many banks were overly reliant on other financial**

institutions as counterparties to their funding and risk management activities. This resulted in excessive risk concentration as numerous financial institutions were too reliant on other large financial institutions for critical operational aspects of their businesses.

- **The failure of Lehman Brothers in September 2008 led to a widespread panic that initially affected Wall Street firms but quickly impacted non-financial businesses as many lost access to funding.** Lehman's deep interconnectedness as a derivatives dealer and uncertainty about potential losses to counterparties led to a broad freeze in markets. Losses on Lehman debt further exacerbated the crisis as it led to a large money market mutual fund (MMF) "breaking the buck" and significant withdrawal requests across the MMF industry. The large withdrawals from MMFs resulted in these entities no longer being able to provide the funding used by many corporations to finance their businesses. Meanwhile, banks saw substantial deposit withdrawals and runs by counterparties. This led to stress that rippled through the financial system and the broader economy.

Obama Administration Actions

The Administration Is Taking Decisive Action to Prevent and Mitigate Excessive Risk-Taking Across the Financial System

- **Regulators are shining a light on the shadow banking system.** Reforms under the Dodd-Frank Act include expanded reporting regarding hedge funds and private equity funds and asset-level disclosures for securitizations. New accounting standards moved off-balance sheet exposures out of the shadows and onto firms' balance sheets. These reforms also allow regulators and investors to better understand the risks that develop in financial firms and across the markets.
- **Reforms put the toughest standards on the largest firms and directly limit interconnectedness.** Wall Street reforms require that the largest, most complex firms meet higher capital, liquidity and risk management standards, giving them incentives to reduce their size and risk. These institutions also must now prepare resolution plans (i.e. living wills) and undergo regular stress tests.

- **The Administration pushed for and the Dodd Frank Act adopted the Volcker Rule to prohibit banks from risky proprietary trading and sponsoring investment funds that are unrelated to serving the bank's core customers' needs.** Recent failures in risk management show the importance of not allowing banks to engage in higher risk, more speculative activities.
- **The FSOC helped create momentum for implementing structural reforms to MMFs.** The FSOC issued for public comment a set of proposed recommendations for MMF reform that was followed by an SEC rule proposal to address risks posed by MMFs.

Five Years Later

- **Many of the elements of the "shadow banking" system have become smaller, posing less risk**. For example, special-purpose investment vehicles (SIVs) used prior to the financial crisis to fund long-term investments by borrowing through short-term commercial paper issuance have virtually disappeared and CDO issuance has fallen materially. Furthermore, the overall asset-backed commercial paper market has shrunk by 78 percent since its peak in 2007 and the triparty repo market has shrunk by nearly 41 percent since its peak in 2008.

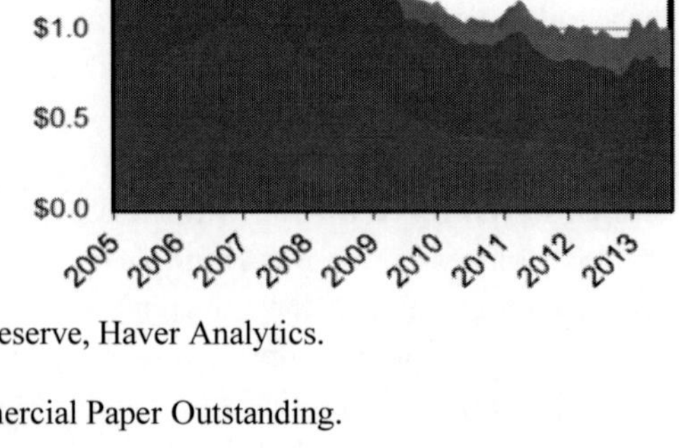

Source: Federal Reserve, Haver Analytics.

Chart 12.1. Commercial Paper Outstanding.

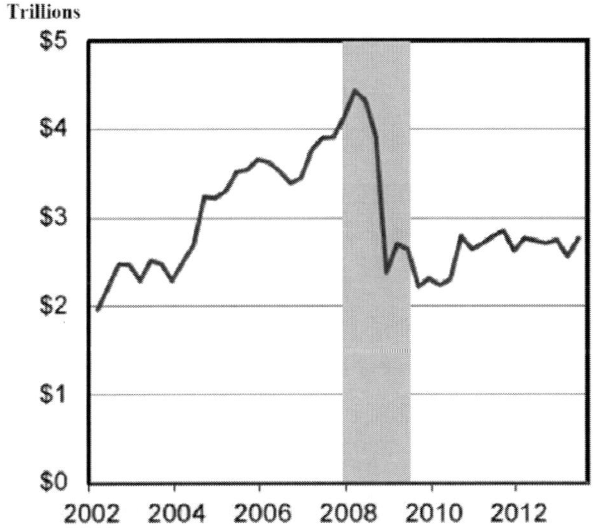

Source: FRBNY, Haver Analytics.
Note: Data prior to April 2008 are estimates based on data provided by clearing banks.

Chart 12.2. Value of Repo Market.

- **Financial firms have reduced their reliance on short term funding by nearly half since 2007.** The share of financial firms' assets supported by less stable wholesale short-term funding has dropped from a peak of 31 percent in 2007 to 17 percent this year.
- **Wall Street Reform is closing gaps in regulation.** The FSOC has now designated two nonbank financial companies – subjecting them to enhanced prudential standards and comprehensive oversight imposed by the Federal Reserve. This standing authority allows the FSOC to identify risks building up outside of the banking system and to require regulation of any nonbank financial company, if the FSOC determines that the company could pose a threat to U.S. financial stability. In addition, the FSOC has designated eight financial market utilities as systemically important subjecting them to enhanced risk-management standards and supervision.
- **The banking regulators remain focused on reducing interconnectedness in the financial sector and reducing complexity at large financial institutions.** The Federal Reserve System has proposed rules covering single counterparty credit limits that are far more robust than the framework that was in place prior to

the crisis. In addition, the Dodd Frank mandate that large firms must develop "living wills" has motivated large financial institutions to reduce their operational complexity.

XIII. Limiting the Impact of Failing Firms

Five Years Ago

- **Poor visibility into financial institutions' exposures to complex structured products made it difficult to accurately assess the risks and liabilities of many financial firms.** The widespread use of derivatives and other shadow banking products allowed many firms to build up substantial off-balance sheet leverage and hidden risks. When the crisis hit, this opaqueness complicated efforts of counterparties, investors, and regulators to understand the risks posed by these financial institutions, and undermined confidence in the broader system.
- **The institutions in our financial system were increasingly interconnected.** As a result, weakness in one institution had the potential to quickly spread to other institutions, including nonbanks such as insurance companies and certain asset managers.
- **Regulators lacked effective resolution tools for large financial institutions facing failure.** Due to the interconnectedness of our financial firms, regulators feared the collapse of a large financial institution could lead to further market disruption and additional failures. This rendered some firms too interconnected and "too big to fail."
- **Without tools to handle the failure of large, complex financial firms, the government facilitated a number of sizable mergers in 2008, further increasing concentration in the sector.** Regulators facilitated a number of bank mergers through the FDIC to avoid disorderly failures of Washington Mutual, Wachovia, and Countrywide. Lacking any resolution authority for nonbank firms, regulators also facilitated the acquisitions of Bear Stearns and Merrill Lynch.
- **The collapse of Lehman Brothers showed the damage that could be caused by the disorderly failure of a complex, interconnected firm.** The September 2008 failure of Lehman Brothers contributed to

widespread panic in the markets and a wholesale run on banks and other sources of funding, including the money market mutual fund (MMF) industry. The collapse of Lehman disrupted short-term funding markets (e.g., MMFs, repo, commercial paper) that were critical to bank operations, and contributed to further declines in asset values that put additional strains on the solvency of our financial system.

Obama Administration Actions

- **The Administration's very first public proposal for Wall Street Reform was for new tools to make sure that no financial firm would be considered "too big to fail."** The Administration's proposal became the Dodd-Frank orderly liquidation authority – a bankruptcy-like approach that allows any financial firm to be liquidated without a threat to financial stability.
- **The Administration worked with Congress to make sure that bailouts would not be allowed by law.** Under the Dodd-Frank orderly liquidation authority, a firm's shareholders are wiped out, culpable management is fired, and creditors, executives, and the financial industry bear the costs – not taxpayers. Dodd-Frank explicitly prohibits the use of taxpayer money to bail out a failing firm.
- **The Administration pursued reforms to prevent further consolidation among U.S. banking firms through acquisitions.** Dodd-Frank incorporates provisions regarding banking acquisitions, including a requirement that the appropriate federal banking agency consider the risks to U.S. financial stability in its review of a banking organization merger, and prohibits banks from merging with or acquiring control of another company if the total consolidated liabilities of the acquiring company upon consummation of the transaction would exceed 10 percent of the liabilities of all financial companies.

Five Years Later

- **Large banks are now required to create "living wills" to provide a roadmap for resolving the firm through bankruptcy.** These comprehensive plans will help regulators wind them down in a rapid and orderly fashion in the event of failure. If the plans are not credible, regulators have the authority to force firms to revise the plans, simplify their businesses, and reduce the risks they pose.
- **New tools have also been put in place to orderly and responsibly resolve failed financial institutions.** Wall Street reforms also established a framework to address the failure of large financial firms when regular bankruptcy is inadequate to mitigate the potential impact on other financial firms and the economy. The FDIC now has the tools to liquidate the assets of a large firm in a responsible manner, similar to the authorities that they have historically been used to successfully resolve insured banks.
- **International regulators have worked together to align standards and coordinate actions in the event of the failure of a large global firm.** Authorities have agreed to key principles for resolving large, complex firms in a coordinated manner. The FDIC has also outlined a resolution strategy intended to minimize global disruptions and facilitate cooperation among international authorities.

XIV. Bank Capital

Five Years Ago

- **The crisis proved that most banks maintained an unacceptably low capital cushion of Tier 1 capital (a measure of high quality, loss absorbing capital).** International bank regulatory agreements required a minimum of 4 percent Tier 1 capital while U.S. capital standards required a minimum of 6 percent Tier 1 to be considered well capitalized.
- **After banks suffered billions of dollars in losses beginning in mid-2007, market participants feared that bank capital levels would prove inadequate to absorb ongoing losses.** In response to the deepening crisis, Treasury deployed TARP resources to inject nearly $250 billion into U.S. banks. However, despite the initial round of

TARP bank investments in fall of 2008, markets remained leery of the continued potential for bank failures.

Obama Administration Actions

- **In February 2009, the Administration announced comprehensive stress tests of the nation's largest banks to ensure that these banks had sufficient capital in order to help stabilize the financial system.** Alongside the stress tests – designed and administered by the Federal Reserve, the FDIC, and the OCC – Treasury indicated any bank found to have an insufficient amount of capital to continue normal operations would be forced to raise capital, preferably from private sources but, if necessary, through a government backstop program that was established.
- **Financial reform has further strengthened capital standards.** The Administration also pushed for higher prudential standards for the largest banks as part of financial reform while also seeking higher capital standards as part of new international banking rules (Basel III).

Five Years Later

- **Bank capital has doubled over the last five years, substantially increasing the stability of the U.S. banking system.** As a result of the combination of stress tests and increasing capital requirements, the largest banks have increased Tier 1 common equity by nearly $450 billion since 2008, doubling their aggregate Tier 1 common equity ratio, from 5.6 percent of risk-weighted assets to 11.1 percent as of mid-2013.
- **U.S. and international standards have significantly increased the quality and quantity of capital banks must now hold. For example:**
  - Basel III has raised the minimum Tier 1 capital ratio from 4 percent to 6 percent, while adding an additional capital buffer of 2.5 percent and a surcharge for the largest, most interconnected firms. It also created a minimum Tier 1 common capital ratio of 4.5 percent, or 7 percent with the capital buffer. The Dodd-Frank

Act also subjects the largest banks to enhanced prudential standards, including additional capital and liquidity requirements.

- The U.S. banking regulators also went a step further by requiring more stringent risk-weights for various categories of assets, which will require banks to hold more capital against the same types and amounts of assets.
- The United States has gone beyond Basel III by proposing supplemental leverage ratios for the largest banks.

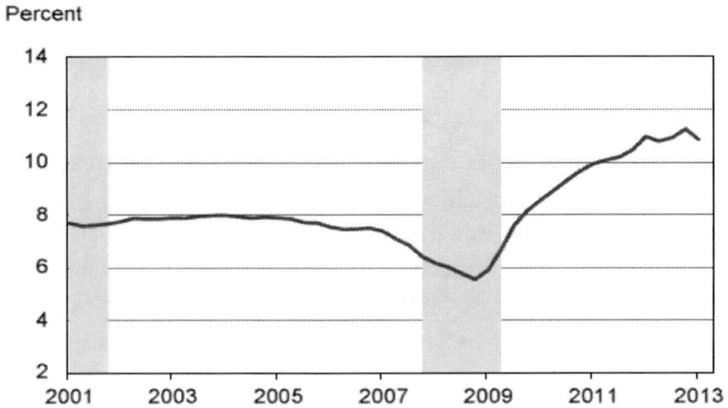

Source: Federal Reserve.

Chart 14.1. Tier 1 Common Capital Ratio for Banks.

- **Banks now hold sufficient capital so that, even under adverse stress test scenarios, they would hold more of it than their actual capital levels in 2008.** Under the severely adverse scenario of the latest stress tests, the estimate of firms' post-stress Tier 1 common capital ratio is more than 2 percentage points higher than their actual capital levels at the end of 2008.

XV. Derivatives

Five Years Ago

- **In the years prior to the financial crisis, over-the-counter (OTC) derivatives, or swaps that are not traded on exchanges, exploded from $95.2 trillion in notional amount at year-end 2000 to $672.6**

trillion in June 2008. In particular, credit default swaps (CDS), a type of derivatives that allows companies to hedge or make bets on certain credit exposures, had grown even more dramatically during this period.

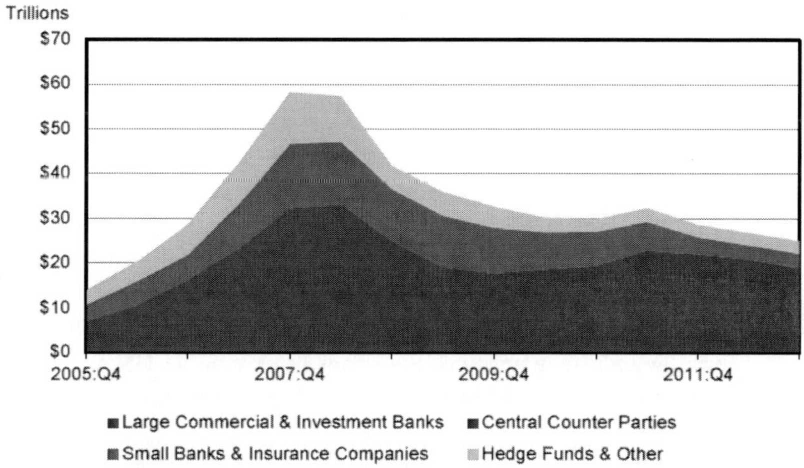

Source: BIS, Haver Analytics.
Note: Notional Amounts Outstanding.

Chart 15.1. Credit Default Swaps Market.

- **OTC derivatives were generally not subject to regulation or transaction reporting, having been exempted from CFTC and SEC regulation by statute.**
- **In September 2008, the failure of Lehman Brothers created substantial disruption in the derivatives markets.** Even more concerning, the substantial CDS exposures of AIG threatened widespread reverberations throughout the marketplace.

Obama Administration Actions

- **To address the risks posed by derivatives, the Administration pushed for fundamental reforms to strengthen the market and oversight of its participants.** Dodd-Frank establishes requirements for major swap dealers and participants to be subject to greater supervision, and requires standardized OTC derivatives be traded on swap execution facilities and centrally cleared, and for data to be reported to repositories to increase transparency and price discovery.

- **Internationally, the Administration pushed, via the G-20, for international agreements to mandate reporting and require central clearing of standardized derivatives, as well as to set capital and margin requirements for non-centrally cleared derivatives.**

Five Years Later

- **The SEC and CFTC have both made substantial progress in implementing the OTC derivatives reforms required by Dodd-Frank by proposing and finalizing key rules.** Swaps trade data repositories have been established, swap execution facilities are forming and the majority of the swaps market in the US is subject to mandatory clearing. These steps have increased transparency and reduced risk in the financial system.
- **International efforts to implement the G-20's commitments to mandate central clearing of standardized OTC derivatives and to require margin requirements for non-centrally cleared derivatives have made substantial progress.** International groups such as the Financial Stability Board (FSB), the Basel Committee, and the International Organization of Securities Commissions (IOSCO) reached agreements on standards regarding the trading and central clearing of OTC derivatives and trade reporting, and the FSB reports that many jurisdictions have adopted legislation implementing some or all of these standards. Furthermore, the global regulatory community just adopted universal standards for margin requirements on non-cleared derivative contracts.

In: After the Financial Crisis
Editor: Edgar I. Bair
ISBN: 978-1-62948-593-5

Chapter 2

ECONOMIC RECOVERY: SUSTAINING U.S. ECONOMIC GROWTH IN A POST-CRISIS ECONOMY*

Craig K. Elwell

SUMMARY

The 2007-2009 recession was long and deep, and according to several indicators was the most severe economic contraction since the 1930s (but still much less severe than the Great Depression). The slowdown of economic activity was moderate through the first half of 2008, but at that point the weakening economy was overtaken by a major financial crisis that would exacerbate the economic weakness and accelerate the decline.

Economic recovery began in mid-2009. Real gross domestic product (GDP) has been on a positive track since then, although the pace has been uneven and slowed significantly in 2011. The stock market has recovered from its lows, and employment has increased moderately. On the other hand, significant economic weakness remains evident, particularly in the balance sheet of households, the labor market, and the housing sector.

Congress was an active participant in the policy responses to this crisis and has an ongoing interest in macroeconomic conditions. Current macroeconomic concerns include whether the economy is in a sustained

* This is an edited, reformatted and augmented version of Congressional Research Service, Publication No. R41332, dated April 18, 2013.

recovery, rapidly reducing unemployment, speeding a return to normal output and employment growth, and addressing government's long-term debt problem.

In the typical post-war business cycle, lower than normal growth during the recession is quickly followed by a recovery period with above normal growth. This above normal growth serves to speed up the reentry of the unemployed to the workforce. Once the economy reaches potential output (and full employment), growth returns to its normal growth path, where the pace of aggregate spending advances in step with the pace of aggregate supply. There is concern that this time the U.S. economy will either not return to its pre-recession growth path but perhaps remain permanently below it, or return to the pre-crisis path but at a slower than normal pace. Problems on the supply side and the demand side of the economy have so far led to a weaker than normal recovery.

If the pace of private spending proves insufficient to assure a sustained recovery, would further stimulus by monetary and fiscal policy be warranted? One lesson from the Great Depression is to guard against a too hasty withdrawal of fiscal and monetary stimulus in an economy recovering from a deep decline.

The removal of fiscal and monetary stimulus in 1937 is thought to have stopped a recovery and caused a slump that did not end until WWII. Opponents of further stimulus maintain that the accumulation of additional government debt would lower future economic growth, but supporters argue that additional stimulus is the appropriate near-term policy.

Moreover, in 2011-2012, the sharply fading effects of fiscal stimulus and weaker growth in Europe have likely dampened economic growth.

In regard to the long-term debt problem, in an economy operating close to potential output, government borrowing to finance budget deficits will in theory draw down the pool of national saving, crowding out private capital investment and slowing long-term growth. However, the U.S. economy is currently operating well short of capacity and the risk of such crowding out occurring is therefore low in the near term. Once the cyclical problem of weak demand is resolved and the economy has returned to a normal growth path, mainstream economists' consensus policy response for an economy with a looming debt crisis is fiscal consolidation—cutting deficits.

Such a policy would have the benefits of low and stable interest rates, a less fragile financial system, improved investment prospects, and possibly faster long-term growth.

BACKGROUND

Severity of the 2008-2009 Recession

The 2008-2009 recession was long and deep, and according to several indicators was the most severe economic contraction since the 1930s (but still much less severe than the Great Depression). The slowdown of economic activity was moderate through the first half of 2008, but at that point the weakening economy was overtaken by a major financial crisis that would exacerbate the economic weakness and accelerate the decline.[1]

When the fall of economic activity finally bottomed out in the second half of 2009, real gross domestic product (GDP) had contracted by approximately 5.1%, or by about $680 billion.[2] At this point the output gap—the difference between what the economy could produce and what it actually produced—widened to an estimated 8.1%. The decline in economic activity was much sharper than in the 10 previous post-war recessions, in which the fall of real GDP averaged about 2.0% and the output gap increased to near 4.0% (see Figure 1). However, the decline falls well short of the experience during the Great Depression, when real GDP decreased by 30% and the output gap probably exceeded 40%.[3]

As output decreased the unemployment rate increased, rising from 4.6% in 2007 to a peak of 10.1% in October 2009. The U.S. unemployment rate has not been at this level since 1982, when in the aftermath of the 1981 recession it reached 10.8%, the highest rate of the post-war period. (During the Great Depression the unemployment rate reached 25%.) This rise in the unemployment rate translates to about 7 million persons put out of work during the recession. Another 8.5 million workers have been pushed involuntarily into part-time employment.[4]

The recession was intertwined with a major financial crisis that exacerbated the negative effects on the economy. Falling stock and house prices led to a large decline in household wealth (net worth), which plummeted by over $16 trillion or about 24% during 2008 and 2009. In addition, the financial panic led to an explosion of risk premiums (i.e., compensation to investors for accepting extra risk over relatively risk-free investments such as U.S. Treasury securities) that froze the flow of credit to the economy, crimping credit supported spending by consumers such as for automobiles, as well as business spending on new plant and equipment.[5]

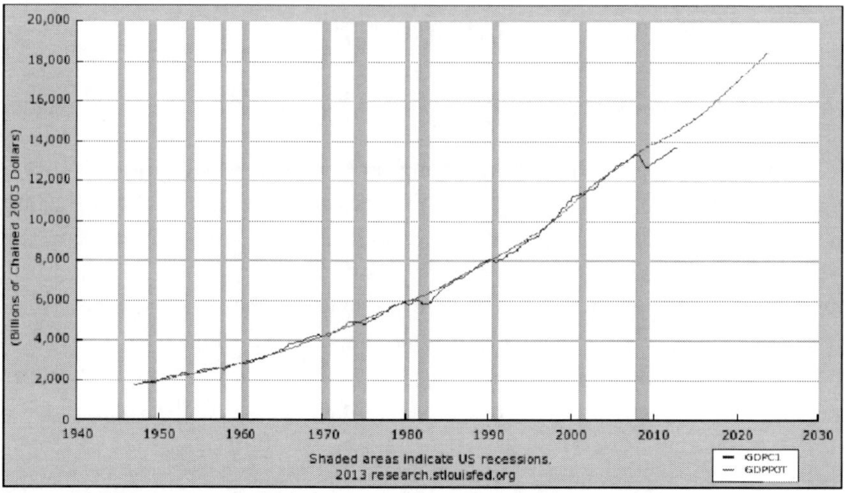

Source: U.S. Department of Commerce: Bureau of Economic Analysis.

Figure 1. Post-War Recessions.

The negative shocks the economy received in 2008 and 2009 were, arguably, more severe than what occurred in 1929. However, unlike in 1929, the severe negative impulses did not turn a recession into a depression, arguably because timely and sizable policy responses by the government helped to support aggregate spending and stabilize the financial system.[6] That stimulative economic policies would have this beneficial effect on a collapsing economy is consistent with standard macroeconomic theory, but without the counterfactual of the economy's path in the absence of these policies, it is difficult to establish with precision how effective these policies were.

Policy Responses to the Financial Crisis and Recession

Both monetary and fiscal policies as well as some extraordinary measures were applied to counter the economic decline. This policy response is thought to have forestalled a more severe economic contraction, helping to turn the economy into the incipient economic recovery by mid-2009. These policies likely continued to stimulate economic activity into 2012.

Monetary Policy Actions

To bolster the liquidity of the financial system and stimulate the economy, during 2008 and 2009 the Federal Reserve (Fed) aggressively applied conventional monetary stimulus by lowering the federal funds rate to near zero and boldly expanding its "lender of last resort" role, creating new lending programs to better channel needed liquidity to the financial system and induce greater confidence among lenders. Following the worsening of the financial crisis in September 2008, the Fed grew its balance sheet by lending to the financial system. As a result, between September and November 2008, the Fed's balance sheet more than doubled, increasing from under $1 trillion to more than $2 trillion.

By the beginning of 2009, demand for loans from the Fed was falling as financial conditions normalized. Had the Fed done nothing to offset the fall in lending, the balance sheet would have shrunk by a commensurate amount, and some of the stimulus that it had added to the economy would have been withdrawn. In the spring of 2009, the Fed judged that the economy, which remained in a recession, still needed additional stimulus.

On March 18, 2009, the Fed announced a commitment to purchase $300 billion of Treasury securities, $200 billion of Agency debt (later revised to $175 billion), and $1.25 trillion of Agency mortgage-backed securities.[7] The Fed's planned purchases of Treasury securities were completed by the fall of 2009 and planned Agency purchases were completed by the spring of 2010. At this point, the Fed's balance sheet stood at just above $2 trillion.[8] (Further monetary policy actions taken to accelerate the pace of economic recovery are discussed later in the report.)

Fiscal Policy Actions

Congress and the Bush Administration enacted the Economic Stimulus Act of 2008 (P.L. 110- 185). This act was a $120 billion package that provided tax rebates to households and accelerated depreciation rules for business. Congress and the Obama Administration passed the American Recovery and Reinvestment Act of 2009 (ARRA; P.L. 111-5). This was a $787 billion package with $286 billion of tax cuts and $501 billion of spending increases that relative to what would have happened without ARRA is estimated to have raised real GDP between 1.5% and 4.2% in 2010 but increased real GDP by progressively smaller amounts in the years that followed.[9]

In terms of extraordinary measures, Congress and the Bush Administration passed the Emergency Economic Stabilization Act of 2008 (P.L. 110-343), creating the Troubled Asset Relief Program (TARP). TARP authorized the Treasury to use up to $700 billion to directly bolster the capital position of banks or to remove troubled assets from bank balance sheets.[10]

Congress was an active participant in the emergence of these policy responses and has an ongoing interest in macroeconomic conditions. Current macroeconomic concerns include whether the economic recovery will be sustained, reducing unemployment, speeding a return to normal output and employment growth, and addressing government's long-term debt situation.

A SUSTAINED BUT SLOW ECONOMIC RECOVERY

The U.S. economy, as measured by real GDP growth (i.e., GDP adjusted for inflation) began to recover in mid-2009. However, the pace of growth over the next 31/2 years was slow and uneven. From the second half of 2009 and through 2010 real GDP increased at an annualized rate of 2.5%. Compared with the early stage of previous post-war economic recoveries, this is a relatively slow pace and much of the economy's upward momentum at this time was sustained by the transitory factors of inventory increases and fiscal stimulus.

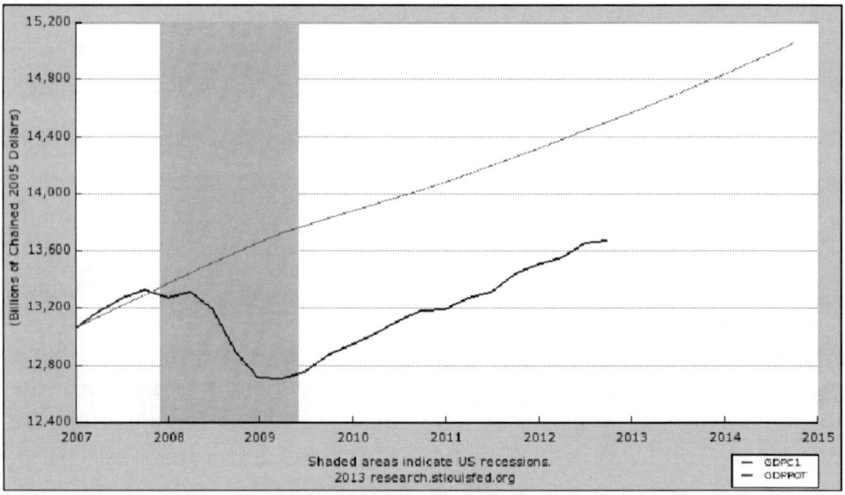

Source: U.S. Department of Commerce: Bureau of Economic Analysis.

Figure 2. Output Gap.

Therefore, sustainable recovery would depend on more enduring sources of demand such spending by consumers and businesses reviving to give continued momentum to the recovery. To a degree, this occurred, but the momentum provided has been lackluster, with the pace of growth decelerating to a 1.8% annualized rate, and the output gap remains sizable (see Figure 2), prompting recurring concerns about the recovery's sustainability.[11]

While business investment spending has been relatively strong during the recovery, consumer spending, typically accounting for two-thirds of final demand, has been relatively weak. Moreover, in 2011-2012, the sharply fading effects of fiscal stimulus and weaker growth in Europe have likely dampened economic growth.[12] Nonetheless, economic activity in the private economy shows signs of slow but steady improvement.

- Credit conditions have improved, making getting loans easier for consumers and businesses, loosening a constraint on many types of credit supported expenditures. The Fed's January 2013 survey of senior loan officers indicated that, on net, bank lending standards and terms continued to ease during the previous three months and that the demand for commercial and industrial loans had increased.[13]
- The stock market has rebounded and interest rate spreads on corporate bonds have narrowed. The Dow Jones stock index, which had plunged to near 6500 in March 2009, by early 2013 had regained all of its lost capitalization. Spreads on investment-grade corporate bonds, a measure of the lenders' perception of risk and creditworthiness of borrowers, have fallen from a high of 600 basis points in December 2008 to near 25 basis points in early 2013.[14]
- Manufacturing activity has shown steady improvement during the recovery. Through February 2013, output had increased 2.0% over a year earlier. Capacity utilization has risen from a low of 64% in mid-2009 to 78.3% in February 2013. (A capacity utilization rate of 80%-85% would be typical for a fully recovered economy.)[15]
- From mid-2009 through February 2013, non-farm payroll employment has increased by about 4 million jobs. Monthly gains have been consistently positive since late 2010, but as evidenced by a weak gain of only 88,000 jobs in March 2013, often not at a scale characteristic of a strong recovery. However, for the 12 months ending in March 2013, monthly employment gains have increased; averaging about 160,000 jobs (see Figure 3).[16]
- The housing sector has recently shown evidence of improving health. Private new housing starts pushed above 900,000 in December 2012, most recently increasing at an annual rate of 917,000 units in February 2013, up from less than 400,000 units during the recession

(see Figure 4). Also, house prices have begun to increase, on average, up about 8% over 12 months ending January 2013.[17]

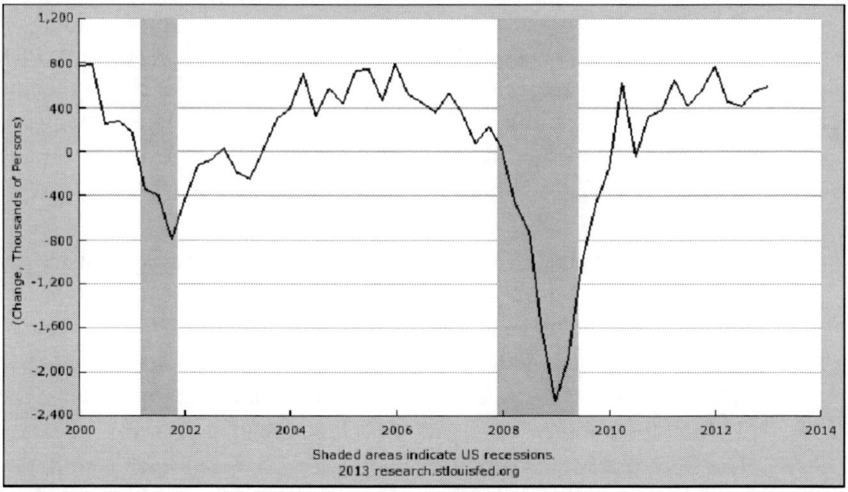

Source: U.S. Department of Labor: Bureau of Labor Statistics.

Figure 3. Monthly Employment Net Gain or Loss.

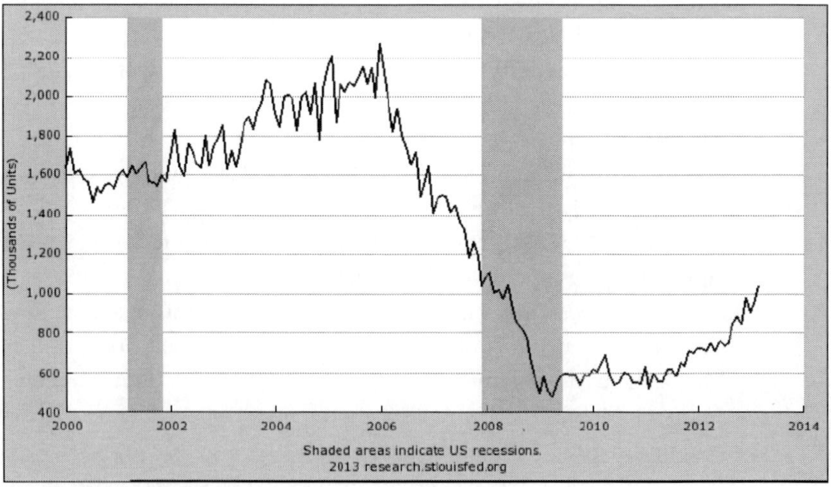

Source: U.S. Department of Commerce: Census Bureau.

Figure 4. Housing Starts.

On the other hand, growth is well below the historical norm for U.S. economic recoveries as persistent sources of economic weakness continue to dampen economic activity.

- Pointing to the slow pace of real GDP growth over 31/2 years of recovery, the output gap had narrowed to only 5.8% of real GDP (see Figure 2).[18]
- Consumer spending, the usual engine of a strong economic recovery, remains tepid, generally slowed by households' ongoing need to rebuild substantial net worth lost during the recession, continued high unemployment and underemployment, and a surge in energy prices in the first half of 2012.
- Employment conditions, despite improvement, remain weak. The unemployment rate, which had peaked at 10.0% in October 2009, has edged down to 7.6% in March 2013, but is still high for this stage of the economic recovery (see Figure 5). A considerable share of the improvement in the unemployment rate is not the result of workers finding jobs, but by discouraged workers leaving the ranks of the officially unemployed by leaving the labor force. The employment to population ratio, which is not affected by changes in labor force participation, has remained near its recession low through three years of economic recovery (see Figure 6). [19] This suggests a labor market that, at best, is only "treading water."
- The housing market, although showing signs of revival, is likely to continue to fall short of its typical contribution to economic recoveries. Although the value of household's financial assets have bounced back since 2009, the value of their real estate assets have not, continuing to dampen consumer spending.[20]
- Growth in the UK and the Euro area has been weak and fiscal austerity measures to stem the growth of public debt have likely pushed the region back into recession, slowing growth further. Slower growth in this region, a major U.S. export market, has likely transmitted a contractionary impulse to the United States, slowing the pace of the U.S. recovery in 2012 and will likely continue to do so into 2013.[21]
- Fiscal policy has tightened significantly since 2010, with federal government expenditures contracting 2.8% in 2011 and 2.2% in 2012, and exerting a dampening effect on economic growth.[22] The current budget debate points to more fiscal tightening in 2013.

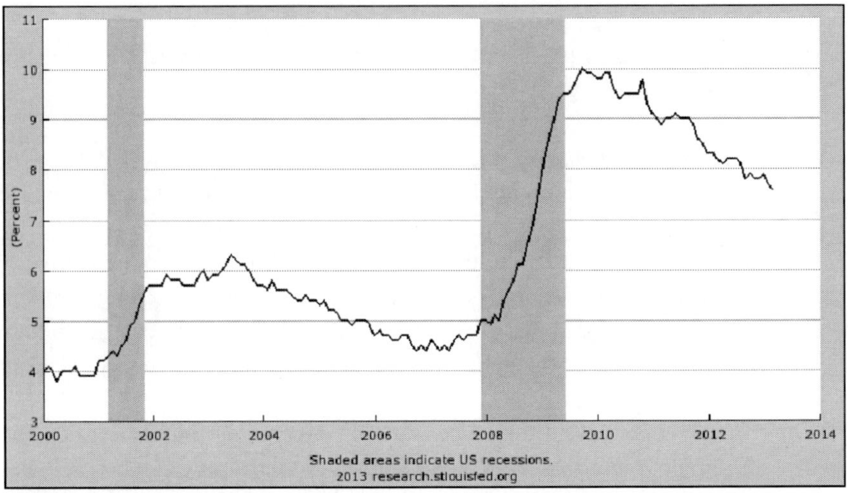

Source: U.S. Department of Labor: Bureau of Labor Statistics.

Figure 5. Unemployment Rate.

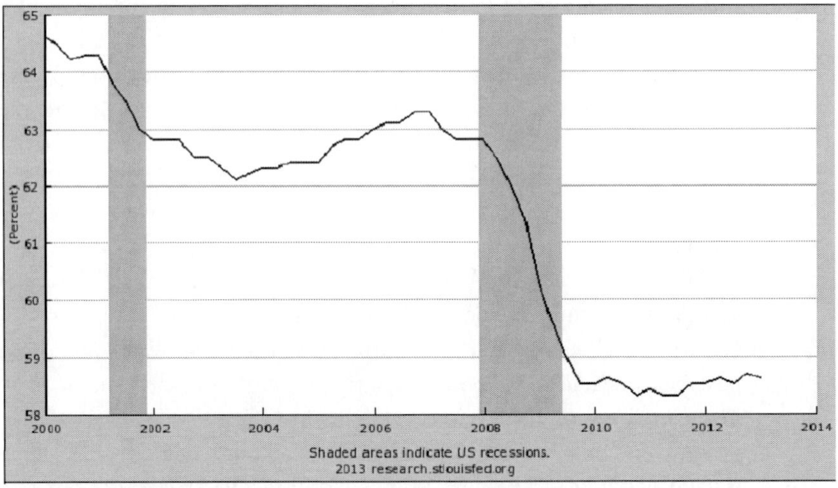

Source: U.S. Department of Labor: Bureau of Labor Statistics.

Figure 6. Employment Population Ratio.

THE SHAPE OF ECONOMIC RECOVERY

In the typical post-war business cycle, lower than normal growth of aggregate demand during the recession is quickly followed by a recovery period with above normal growth of spending, perhaps spurred by some degree of monetary and fiscal stimulus. The degree of acceleration of growth in the first two to three years of recovery has varied across post-war business cycles, but has been at an annual pace in a range of 4% to 8%.[23] This above normal growth brings the economy back more quickly to the pre-recession growth path, and speeds up the reentry of the unemployed to the workforce.

Once the level of aggregate demand approaches the level of potential GDP (or full employment), the economy returns to its pre-recession growth path, where the growth of aggregate spending is slower because it is constrained by the growth of aggregate supply, which in recent years is estimated to have been at an annual pace of near 3.0%. (A subsequent section of the report looks more closely at aggregate supply.)[24]

There is concern, however, that this time the U.S. economy, without supporting stimulus from policy actions, will either not return to its pre-recession growth path, perhaps remain permanently below it, or return to the pre-crisis path but at a slower than normal pace, or worse, dip into a second recession. Below normal growth would almost certainly translate into below normal recovery of employment, whereas a second round of recession could increase the already high unemployment rate. The next sections of this report discuss problems on the supply side and the demand side of the economy that could lead to a weaker than normal recovery.

Demand Side Problems?

Much of the vigor that occurred on the demand side of the economy in 2009 and 2010 appears to have come from fiscal stimulus and business inventory restocking. Fiscal stimulus and inventory rebuilding are, however, temporary sources of support of aggregate spending. Sooner or later fiscal stimulus falls away. The Congressional Budget Office (CBO) projects that fiscal stimulus peaked in 2010, provided a smaller boost to demand in 2011, and continued to diminish to a negligible force by the end of 2012.[25] Inventory building is a self-limiting process that will not go on indefinitely; stock-building was weaker during most of 2011, and despite a stronger turn in late

2011 and early 2012, inventory growth will unlikely continue to have a major positive effect on aggregate demand.

A strong recovery of private sector demand, including consumer spending, investment spending, and exports, is required to sustain an economic recovery that brings the economy quickly back to its pre-recession growth path and unemployment rate. However, there are major uncertainties about the potential medium-term strength of each of these components that could dampen aggregate spending and constrain the economy's ability to generate a recovery period with above normal growth and quickly falling unemployment.

Consumption Spending

Personal consumption expenditures historically constitute the largest and most stable component of aggregate spending in the U.S. economy. During the first three post-war decades, personal consumption spending averaged a 62% share of GDP. However, that share rose significantly over the next three decades, averaging about 65% in the 1980s, 67% during the 1990s, and about 70% between 2001 and 2007. The high level of household spending reached during the 2001-2007 expansion is unlikely to reemerge during the current recovery because it was supported by an unsustainable increase in household debt, a decrease in personal savings, ease of access to credit, and lower energy prices.

Household Debt

In the mid-1980s, after a long period of relative stability at a scale of around 45% to 50% of GDP, the debt level of households began to rise steadily, reaching over 100% of GDP by 2008. Such a substantial rise in the level of household debt was sustainable so long as rising home prices and a rising stock market continued to also increase the value of household net worth, and interest rates remained low, countering the rise in the burden of debt service as a share of income.

The collapse of the housing and stock markets in 2008 and 2009 substantially decreased household net worth, which had, by mid-2009, fallen about $16 trillion below its 2007 peak of nearly $67 trillion.[26] This near 25% fall in net worth pushed the household debt burden up substantially. Unlike in earlier post-war recoveries, the need of households to repair their damaged balance sheets induced a large diversion of current income from consumption spending to debt reduction.[27] Since 2008, households have reduced their outstanding debt about $1 trillion. [28] If debt reduction continues in 2013, it is likely to be a continuing drag on the pace of economic recovery.

A substantial rebuilding of household net worth has occurred during the recovery. Through the fourth quarter of 2012, household net worth has increased by about $15 trillion from its 2009 trough, reaching about $66 trillion and recovering nearly 95% of what was lost during the recession. This improvement has occurred largely on the asset side of the household balance sheet and primarily for financial assets due to the rise of the stock market from its low point in early 2009.[29] Such gains tend to be concentrated in higher-income households and not a major source of wealth for the average household. Traditionally, rising home equity, largely dependent on the path of house prices, has been the major contributor to household wealth. The rapid rise of home prices during the last economic expansion caused an equally rapid rise in home equity. Consumers borrowed against this equity to fund current spending. With the sharp fall of home prices, home equity was reduced substantially, erasing that source of funding. Home prices are only now beginning to rise and the housing market is expected to remain relatively weak for several more years, slowing the pace of households rebuilding this component of their net worth, and continuing to dampen the pace consumer spending (see Figure 7).[30]

In addition to diverting more personal income to saving, a continued weak labor market is likely to dampen income growth and, in turn, slow the recovery of consumer spending.

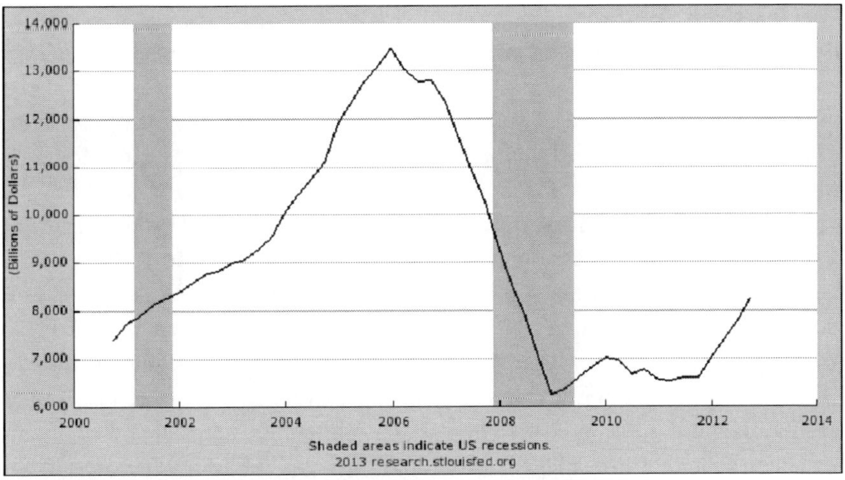

Source: Board of Governors of the Federal Reserve System.

Figure 7. Household Equity in Real Estate.

Credit Conditions

Easy credit availability in the pre-crisis economy enabled households to readily borrow against their rising home equity to fund added spending. Financial innovations allowed lenders to keep interest rates low and offer liberal terms and conditions to entice households to borrow. Many believe that credit conditions will remain tighter during the current expansion. Interest rates are still historically low, but banks greatly tightened the terms and conditions of consumer loans during the crisis and recession and have only slowly relaxed them as the recovery has proceeded. While not likely as important a driver of higher savings as high household debt, tighter credit conditions will make it less likely that households will exploit any increase in their home equity to fund current spending, further constraining consumer spending relative to what occurred during the 2001-2007 economic expansion.

Personal Saving

The U.S. personal saving rate averaged about 10% of GDP consistently through the 1970s, 1980s, and 1990s. Subsequently, the personal saving rate declined sharply, reaching a low of 1.0% by 2005.[31] It is likely that the reduction of household saving was in large measure a consequence of the sizable increase in household net worth associated with increased house prices and stock prices occurring at that time. As wealth rose rapidly, it was less urgent to divert current income to saving.

The sharp reduction of household net worth during the recent recession dramatically changed the financial circumstances of households, reducing the use of debt-financed spending. The need to repair household balance sheets induced households to pay down debt. The poor prospect for the appreciation of house prices has eliminated the ability to use rising equity as a substitute for saving.

In addition, the increase in economic uncertainty in the aftermath of the financial crisis and recession will likely mean that over the medium term, households could continue to be more inclined to save. As the economic decline intensified, the personal saving rate increased, climbing from 3.5% of GDP in 2007 to 6.1% of GDP at the bottom of the recession in 2009.[32] However, with economic recovery the personal saving rate has fallen, averaging about 3.8% in 2012. The passing of the dire financial and economic circumstances that prevailed in 2008 and 2009 has likely led to some of the recent moderation in households' saving behavior. A lower rate of saving enables higher rates of consumption, but it is uncertain that continued fall of the saving rate will be a substantial source of support for current spending by households.

Energy Prices

A 30% increase in the price of oil from October 2011 through April 2012 adversely affected household budgets and likely contributed to the slow rate of increase in consumer spending over the same period.[33] In the short run, the U.S. demand for energy is relatively inelastic, with little curtailment of energy use in the face of the rising price. As households and businesses spend more for energy, which is largely imported, they tend to spend less on domestic output, slowing economic growth.[34] Since April 2012, the price of oil decreased and appears to have stabilized at about 10% below this peak. If it remains near the current level, the dampening effect on economic growth is likely to fade. In addition, increasing supplies of shale gas have resulted in lower natural gas prices, which may benefit household budgets.

Slow Recovery of Consumer Spending?

If consumer spending continues its slow paced recovery, then for the U.S. economy to return to its normal pre-crisis growth path, an improved pace of GDP growth will have to come from other components of aggregate demand: investment spending, net exports, or government spending.

Investment Spending

Investment spending is the third-largest component of aggregate spending, historically averaging 17% to 18% of GDP in years of near normal output growth. (Government spending is second largest at about 20%.) Historically, the largest portion of total investment spending is business fixed investment, its share averaging 11% to 12% of GDP in periods of normal growth. The second component of total investment is residential investment (i.e., new housing), averaging 4% to 5% of GDP.

Investment spending is very sensitive to economic conditions and more volatile than consumer spending. This sensitivity is at least in part because investment projects are often postponable to a time when economic conditions are more favorable. Its volatility makes investment spending an important determinant of the amplitude, down and up, of the typical business cycle.[35]

As aggregate spending fell and credit availability tightened in 2008, investment spending quickly weakened. As a share of real GDP, investment spending fell from about 16% in 2007 to about 11% at the economy's trough in 2009. The sharp fall in real GDP from the second quarter of 2008 through the first quarter of 2009 was nearly fully accounted for by the sharp fall of investment spending over this same period. Throughout the economic recovery, investment spending has been a leading source of economic growth, elevating its share of real GDP to 12.7% in 2010, 13.5% in 2011, and 14% in 2012.[36]

In particular, the *equipment and software* component of nonresidential investment has been the principal source of business spending strength and an important contributor to the pace of the economic recovery. Equipment and software spending increased 14.6% in 2010, contributing nearly a full percentage point to the growth of real GDP in that year. This category of business investment spending continued to be an important source of economic growth in 2011, increasing at an annual rate of 11.0% and contributing 0.7 percentage points to real GDP growth. However, in 2012, investment spending on equipment and software slowed, advancing at a 6.9% annual rate and contributing 0.5 percentage points to real GDP growth.[37]

Typically, this same sensitivity also works in the opposite direction. Strongly rising investment spending, responding to improving market demand, reduced uncertainty, and expanding credit availability, often gives an above normal contribution to the rebound of aggregate spending during the recovery phase of the business cycle.

Looking forward, however, some significant constraints on both residential and business investment raise uncertainty about whether investment spending will continue to be a strong contributor to economic recovery, and therefore, whether it could be a component of aggregate spending capable of compensating for a weaker than normal recovery of spending by consumers.

The principal constraint on residential investment has been the large inventory of vacant housing, left over from the 2002-2006 housing boom. It is estimated that the number of vacancies could be more than 2 million units above what would normally be expected at this stage of the business cycle.[38] As discussed above, the housing market has recently shown signs of stabilizing, and residential investment spending has risen strongly in 2012, albeit from a very low base. On balance new house construction is likely to remain relatively weak for the next two years while the inventory overhang continues to be worked down.

The prospect for nonresidential investment is likely to be better than for residential investment, but it is not clear that with economic recovery nonresidential investment will exceed its pre-crisis level. On the supply side, capacity utilization rates have climbed back from record lows of below 70% reached during the recession, but, at about 78% currently, are still only near the lows reached in the 1990 and the 2001 recessions and well short of the 80% to 85% that would typically correspond to operating near or at capacity.[39] On the demand side, business investment in new plants and equipment is most often a response to the expectation of increased demand for the products they produce. The main driver of that demand is consumer spending and, as discussed above, that spending has been tepid, with the not unlikely prospect that it may continue to be weak over the near term if households have made a lasting commitment to increased savings.

Stronger foreign demand could also stimulate investment spending and in theory compensate for the weaker pull of domestic demand, but as discussed more fully below, foreign demand may also be weak. Also, problems in the financial sector have caused sharply reduced activity in commercial real estate, contributing to persistent weakness in business investment spending on structures.[40]

In general, it seems questionable whether total investment spending would provide the offset to a below normal contribution of consumption spending to economic growth over the near term.

Net Exports

The U.S. trade deficit (real net exports) shrank from about 6% of real GDP in 2006 to below 3% in 2009. Since the beginning of the recession in late 2007 through the end of the contraction in mid-2009, net exports have made a significant positive contribution to real GDP in an otherwise declining economy. Even as economic weakness abroad caused U.S. exports to fall, imports fell by more, providing a net positive push to current economic activity.[41]

The 3 percentage point swing in real net exports is, however, largely the consequence of the severe economic weakness in the United States over this period. Since mid-2009, the deficit in net exports has decreased very little, falling slightly to 2.9% of real GDP in 2012. This relatively flat performance means that over the course of the current recovery net exports have not had either a substantial positive or negative impact on economic growth. This neutral pattern makes it uncertain that net exports can be expected to boost aggregate spending sufficiently to offset weak consumption over the medium term and help assure a sustained recovery at a pace that steadily reduces unemployment.

Boosting U.S. Net Exports through a Rebalancing of Global Spending

Increasing U.S. net exports to any degree requires that the trade deficit continues to decrease. For that to happen, trade surpluses of the rest of the world with the United States must also decrease. To achieve this adjustment of trade flows, a sizable rebalancing of domestic and external demand on the part of the deficit and surplus economies would need to occur.[42]

Because a trade deficit is a consequence of an economy spending more than it produces, rebalancing in this circumstance requires a decrease of domestic spending and increase of domestic saving. In contrast, for overseas trade partners, because a trade surplus is a consequence of an economy spending less than it produces, rebalancing in this circumstance requires an increase of trade partner domestic spending and decrease in trade partner domestic saving.

This rebalancing of spending will put pressure on the dollar to depreciate and foreign currencies to appreciate. A fall in the value of the dollar relative to the currencies of the surplus countries causes the price of foreign goods to rise for U.S. buyers and the price of U.S. goods to fall for foreign buyers. This change in the relative price of foreign versus domestic goods will cause the net exports of the United States to rise, giving the boost in spending needed to potentially offset reduced consumption spending. The change in relative prices would also cause the net exports of surplus countries to fall as more of current output is absorbed by increased domestic spending.

In the United States, as discussed above, some measure of rebalancing seems to be occurring, as evidenced by the increase in the personal saving rate above its pre-recession low. Although there are good reasons to expect this increase to be sustained, there is the possibility that households would eventually revert to their pre-crisis low saving patterns. However, even if household saving remains higher, it is likely that any significant increase in the overall U.S. national saving rate would also require an increase in government saving via smaller federal budget deficits.

Large U.S. budget deficits over the near term are providing a needed boost to weak aggregate spending during the early stages of an economic recovery. With the strengthening of private spending as the recovery matures, large government budget deficits would fade away, causing government saving to rise. What puts this fading away of budget deficits in doubt over the long term is the prospect of having to fund the obligations attached to the rising demand of an aging U.S. population for healthcare, Social Security, and other entitlements. Without policy actions to address these long-term demands, it is not clear how the long-term budget deficits will fall.

Effective global rebalancing arguably also involves sizable adjustments by the largest surplus economies—Germany, Japan, and China. However, there are significant potential constraints on how substantially each of these three economies can "save less and spend more," perhaps limiting any sizable appreciation of their currencies relative to the dollar, and any associated boost in U.S. net exports.

The inability of Germany to move its exchange rate independently from the other Euro area economies reduces its flexibility of adjustment. In addition, the effects of the 2008-2009 recession have left limited room for further fiscal expansion and small ability to lower the household saving rate. In addition, the ongoing sovereign debt crisis in the euro area has dampened growth prospects in Germany, likely weakening the demand for U.S. exports. Although its level of debt is not high, recent German policy actions have stressed fiscal consolidation, tending to increase saving and dampen spending.[43] Japan, which does have a very high level of public debt, has little to no room for fiscal expansion and a poor prospect of boosting household spending. Moreover, both Germany and Japan, faced with substantial near-term economic weakness in the aftermath of the global recession, may take steps to avoid the dampening of their net exports that a sizable appreciation of the exchange rate would cause.

China has the largest bilateral trade surplus with the United States and therefore has the potential to have a large impact on U.S. export sales and through that a significant positive impulse on the pace of the U.S. economic recovery. Also, economic growth has remained relatively strong in China through the recent global financial crisis and recession, and aggregate demand is expected to be strong through the next two to three years. What is uncertain, however, is whether a greater share of this spending will be domestic demand, particularly consumption spending by Chinese households.

The very high rate of saving by Chinese households is thought to be a precautionary measure to compensate for a lack of social insurance. It likely also reflects limited access to consumer credit. The difficulty for the near-term task of sustaining economic recovery is that even if policy actions are taken to remove these constraints on consumer spending, households are likely to only gradually change their pattern of consumption and not provide a sharp near-term boost to domestic spending.

Also, a closer look at the sources of increase in China's domestic saving over the last decade reveals that the principal contributor to that growth was Chinese companies, not households. Therefore, changing the saving practices of Chinese companies is likely to be an important aspect of any large increase in China's saving rate. It is argued by some that Chinese companies retain too large a share of their earnings. Better access to credit and changes in the governance rules of Chinese business would likely reduce the business saving rate. But, as with households, even if such policy initiatives are forthcoming, the change in the business saving rate is likely to emerge only gradually.[44]

Even with a successful rebalancing, it is unlikely that China alone can propel a boost in U.S. net exports sufficient to offset weak domestic demand and pace economic recovery. China's global trade surplus is estimated to be about 10% of GDP. However, China is only about one-third the size of the U.S. economy. Therefore, if China's trade were only with the United States, it would have to reduce its trade surplus by 3% of GDP to effect a 1 percentage point reduction of the U.S. trade deficit. But since, in fact, only about 16% of China's trade is with the United States, it would take a 15 percentage point change in China's trade balance (moving from a surplus equal to 10% of GDP to a deficit equal to 5% of GDP) to reduce the U.S. trade deficit by 1 percentage point. (This assumes that the fall of China's trade surplus is not offset by an increase of other trading partners' surpluses.)

Other emerging Asian economies also run trade surpluses, and adding these to the calculation makes the relative scale of rebalancing needed to achieve a given amount of improvement in the U.S trade deficit more feasible. However, all of emerging Asia is only about half the size of the U.S. economy. Therefore, if the U.S. share of the whole region's trade is similar to China's, emerging Asia would need to accomplish a sizable 7 percentage point change in its trade balance to generate a 1 percentage point change in the U.S. trade balance. As with China, for a reduction of the trade surpluses of other emerging Asian economies to happen quickly, their currencies will need to appreciate against the dollar.

All in all, there are reasons to doubt whether U.S. net exports can increase over the near term at a pace sufficient to fully compensate for the prospect of slower than normal growth of other components of U.S. domestic spending.

Supply Side Problems?

The supply side of the economy governs its capacity for producing goods and services. That capacity is a function of the economy's supplies of labor and capital and the level of technology used to turn labor and capital into the output of goods and services. In the short run, the potential supplies of these productive factors are relatively fixed and will determine the economy's potential output. In periods of economic slack, rising aggregate demand can increase the economy's output and employment up to the level of potential output, which corresponds with full employment.

In the long run, as the supplies of capital and labor and the level of technology increase, the level of potential output also increases. Over time the steady rise of potential output will define the economy's long-term growth path (called the "trend" growth rate). When aggregate demand is below potential output the economy can grow faster than trend growth, but when the level of aggregate demand reaches the level of potential output, further growth of output will be constrained to the trend growth rate.

Typically the long-run growth path is thought to be relatively stable and not greatly affected by recessions and the associated short-term fluctuations in aggregate demand. Over the post-war period, the average annual growth rate of potential output for the United States has been 3.4%; however, since the 1970s it has averaged closer to 3.0%.[45]

An analysis by the International Monetary Fund (IMF) examines the question of whether output will return to its pre-crisis trend.[46] It examines the medium-term and long-run paths of output after 88 banking crises over the past four decades in a wide range of countries (including both advanced and developing economies). A key conclusion was that seven years after the crisis, output had declined relative to trend by nearly 10% for the average country. But there was considerable variation of outcomes across crisis episodes.

In other words, such crises not only reduce actual output, but also may reduce potential output (the economy's structural and institutional capacity to produce output). In this circumstance, the economy could return to its trend growth rate, but there is unlikely to be a rebound period of above normal growth to quickly return the economy to its pre-crisis potential output and growth path and, in turn, quickly reduce unemployment. This failure to return to the pre-crisis potential output means that the economy bears the burden of a permanent output loss and the large initial increase in the unemployment rate caused by the crisis could persist even as the economy is growing at its trend rate.

The IMF analysis suggests that the reduction of the post-crisis growth path is likely to be the consequence of decreases of approximately equal size in the employment rate, the capital-labor ratio, and productivity. The adverse effect of the financial crisis on the employment rate is thought to arise from an increase in the "structural unemployment rate," hampering the post-crisis economy's ability to accomplish the needed reallocation of labor from sectors that have contracted permanently to sectors that are expanding.

Because the aftermath of the crisis will likely involve sizable changes in the composition of the economy, it likely also increases the mismatch between the skills of the unemployed and the skills demanded in the post-crisis labor market—job vacancies go unfilled for lack of a worker with sufficient skills for the job.[47] Also, labor force participation rates may fall if the crisis is severe enough to substantially increase the numbers of the long-term unemployed, some of whom may become discouraged from searching for a new job. A crisis-induced fall of house prices and a rising incidence of mortgages with negative equity will also discourage the geographic mobility of workers who are unable to sell their houses.

The adverse impact of a financial crisis on capital accumulation is likely the combined outcome of several factors. Decreased demand for products and heightened uncertainty of potential return dampens the incentive to invest. In addition, the financial crisis could impede the process of financial intermediation for up to several years, as weakened balance sheets, lower collateral values, and elevated risk premiums slow the flow of credit and elevate the real cost of borrowing.

The dampening effect on productivity may occur as higher risk premiums and a generally more cautious approach to spending by businesses diminish the willingness and ability to finance relatively high-risk projects. Expenditures on research and development are typically pro-cyclical and likely to be sharply reduced in times of crisis.

Productivity tends to recover quickly after recessions and thus allows the economy to resume growth at the pre-crisis trend rate. However, the capital and employment losses tend to endure and keep the economy on a lower growth path.

Has the recent financial crisis caused a reduction in the potential output of the U.S. economy and placed it on a lower trend growth path? It is difficult to make a concurrent determination because potential output is not directly observable, and can only be imputed from the economy's actual post-crisis performance. A clear determination of any such permanent output loss is some years in the future.

Although the IMF study gives reasons why the financial crisis possibly could have adversely affected the economy's supply side, the study also finds that there can be some significant mitigating factors that could be particularly relevant for the U.S. economy. First, a high pre-crisis investment share is a good predictor of a large potential output loss. This is a reflection of the high sensitivity of investment to the negative effects of a financial crisis. For the United States there was no sharp increase in investment spending above trend as measured as a share of GDP for the three years prior to the financial crisis, averaging near a typical 16% of GDP.[48]

Second, the IMF study also found that those economies that aggressively apply stimulative fiscal and monetary policies during the crisis tend to have smaller medium-term output losses. As already discussed, the United States has applied quickly and substantially stimulative polices in response to the financial crisis.

Third, countries with fewer labor market rigidities suffered smaller medium-term output losses. U.S. labor markets, as compared with other advanced economies, are relatively free of labor market rigidities, though as mentioned declining house prices may have reduced mobility of some workers who own their own homes.

The Congressional Budget Office (CBO) currently projects U.S. potential output to increase at an annual average rate of 2.2% for the 2013-2018 period, the same pace as during the 2002-2012 period. CBO's projected rate of growth of potential output is well below the post-war average of 3.3%. Slower growth of potential GDP is largely the consequence of a projection of significantly slower labor force growth than during the post-war period in the coming decades. Most of the slowdown in labor force growth is related to long-term demographic changes forced by an aging population; however, a protracted recession with growing numbers of long-term unemployed and discouraged workers has also contributed to this labor force dynamic.[49]

Policy Responses to Increase the Pace of Economic Recovery

The momentum of the current economic recovery has been assisted by injections of fiscal and monetary stimulus. But with substantial economic slack remaining and with unemployment still stubbornly high, would further stimulus by monetary and fiscal policy be warranted to sustain economic recovery?

Fiscal Policy Actions Taken during the Recovery

In 2010, many economists argued that another dose of fiscal stimulus was warranted because the effects of the first stimulus package were beginning to fade, and because of evidence that private spending lacked sufficient vigor to sustain a healthy recovery.[50] In this situation, the risk of not applying further fiscal stimulus could be several years of sub-normal growth, or worse, dipping into a second recession.

In response to concerns that the recovery was faltering, Congress passed and President Obama signed in December 2010 the Tax Relief, Unemployment Insurance Reauthorization, and Job Creation Act of 2010 (P.L. 111-312). The essential features of that measure were an extension for two years of the "Bush" tax cuts, a 2 percentage point cut in the payroll tax during 2011, a 13- month extension of unemployment benefits, and allowance for more rapid expensing of business investment in 2011. The CBO estimated that the direct stimulative effect of these revenue and spending changes as measured by the increase in the federal budget deficit would be approximately $374 billion in 2011 and $422 billion in 2012.[51]

A major counterforce to federal stimulus policies during this recovery has been the contraction of spending by state and local governments. Direct expenditures by state and local governments decreased 1.8% in 2010, 3.4%% in 2011, and 1.4% in 2012, and subtracting from real GDP growth 0.2 percentage points in 2010, 0.4 percentage points in 2011, and 0.2 percentage points in 2012.[52]

In 2013, federal fiscal policy has reversed course and tightened, exerting a drag on the recovery. This fiscal tightening results from automatic spending cuts, enacted by the Budget Control Act of 2011(P.L. 112-25), and the expiration at the end of 2012 of the 2 percentage point cut in payroll taxes and of tax rate cuts for incomes above certain thresholds. CBO estimates that this fiscal tightening will cause economic growth in 2013 to be 1.5 percentage points below what it otherwise would be.[53]

Evaluating the Case for Fiscal Stimulus

Fiscal stimulus is not without its critics. The case against more fiscal stimulus comes in three forms, used separately or in combination: one, no further stimulus is needed; two, fiscal stimulus does not work; and three, stimulus increases the budget deficit, makes the U.S. long-term debt problem worse, and dampens economic growth.[54]

In regard to the need for stimulus, the U.S. economy does have strong recuperative powers and it is possible that private spending and economic growth will soon surge without further fiscal stimulus. Events such as improved consumer confidence, lower energy prices, a more normal flow of credit, or faster growth in the rest of the world could separately or in combination induce stronger spending by households and businesses. However, given the severity of the recent recession and, as outlined above, given the current weakness of private spending and the several economic obstacles that households and businesses will probably continue to face over the near term, there remains a significant risk of sub-normal growth for the next several years.

In regard to the ability of fiscal stimulus to boost output and employment, some economists argue that fiscal stimulus only shifts spending, it does not increase spending. In this view, when people see the government running a budget deficit, they anticipate that the government will need to increase taxes in the future to pay off the debt. This anticipation causes households and businesses to increase their current savings to pay for the higher taxes. The increase in saving tends to offset the stimulative effect of the budget deficit.[55] There is little empirical support for this theory, however. Mainstream economic analysis indicates that in circumstances like the present, in which the economy's output is likely constrained by insufficient demand, fiscal stimulus can raise the level of output and employment.[56]

In regard to the long-term debt problem, it is often pointed out that for an economy operating close to potential output, government borrowing to finance budget deficits will draw down the pool of national saving, leaving less available to support private capital investment. Private investment by business and households in education, housing, research and development, and capital equipment that would have otherwise occurred is in theory "crowded out" through higher interest rates bid up by government borrowing. If budget deficits divert national saving from private investment, other things equal, future productivity and income growth may be slowed.

However, the U.S. economy is currently operating well short of capacity and market interest rates are generally at or near historical lows, making the risk of such "crowding out" occurring and damaging future economic growth not seem immediate.[57] Another variant of this argument against fiscal stimulus maintains that by increasing public debt, fiscal stimulus undermines household and business confidence and causes them to postpone current spending. In this view, contrary to mainstream economic thinking, shrinking the deficit would, by improving confidence, actually stimulate current spending by consumers and business.[58]

The Short-Term and Long-Term Fiscal Problems

Because the United States faces two macroeconomic problems, two policy responses are, arguably, appropriate: a short-term policy to sustain a cyclical recovery of economic growth and a long-term policy to trim government debt. Conceptually there is no necessary tradeoff between these two objectives. They can be mutually reinforcing: a credible commitment to dealing with the long-term debt problem allays investor uncertainty and increases the near-term incentive to spend, while effectively dealing with the short-term problem of weak aggregate demand puts the economy on a stronger growth path, which boosts tax revenue and eases the long-term debt problem.

Once the short-term problem of weak demand is solved and the economy has returned to a normal growth path, the appropriate policy response for an economy with a looming debt crisis is arguably fiscal consolidation—cutting deficits. Such a policy is thought to have the benefits of low and stable interest rates, a less fragile financial system, improved investment prospects, and possibly faster long-term growth.

To address the government's long-term fiscal problem, Congress passed on August 2, 2011, the Budget Control Act of 2011 (P.L. 112-25). The Budget Control Act (BCA) sets caps on discretionary spending. It also created the Congressional Joint Select Committee on Deficit Reduction, whose task was to propose further policy changes that would lead to $1.5 trillion in further deficit reduction over 10 years. The joint committee was unable to reach an agreement on how to achieve further deficit reduction. In the absence of an agreement, the BCA established a process for automatic spending reduction.[59]

Monetary Policy Actions Taken during the Recovery

On November 3, 2010, the Fed announced that it would provide more monetary stimulus by means of the purchase an additional $600 billion of Treasury securities at a pace of about $75 billion per month, and continue the practice of replacing maturing securities with Treasury security purchases. When this second round of monetary stimulus (sometimes referred to as "quantitative easing 2" or QE2)[60] was completed in June 2011, the Fed had increased the size of its balance sheet to more than $2.5 trillion. The maturity lengths of the securities purchased were mostly between 21/2 and 10 years.[61]

The Fed argued at that time that a second dose of monetary stimulus was needed because economic growth is decelerating and much of what economic momentum existed was being provided by the transitory factors of inventory adjustment and fiscal stimulus. In the second half of 2010, growth slowed to around 2%, a pace barely fast enough to keep the unemployment rate from rising. Fed Chairman Ben Bernanke indicated that of particular concern was the substantial increase in the share of the long-term unemployed (workers who have been without work for six months or more). Such long-term unemployment tends to convert temporary cyclical unemployment into more intractable structural unemployment. In addition, the lingering economic slack in the economy had added to deflationary pressure. Measures of core inflation had been decelerating during 2010, reaching a low of only slightly above 1%.

A continuous decline in the price level is troublesome because in a weak or contracting economy it can lead to a damaging, self-reinforcing, downward spiral of prices and economic activity. Deflation exacerbated the economy's decline during the Great Depression.[62]

To support a stronger recovery, the Fed announced on September 21, 2011, that it would purchase by the end of June 2012 $400 billion of Treasury securities with remaining maturities of 6 years to 30 years and to sell an equal amount of Treasury securities with remaining maturities of 3 years or less.[63] In June 2012, the Fed announced that it would extend this program through the end of 2012. This program does not expand the size of the Fed's balance sheet. Rather, by changing the composition of its asset holdings toward longer maturities, the Fed is attempting to put downward pressure on longer-term interest rates and increase monetary policy's stimulative effect on economic activity.[64]

On September 13, 2012, the Fed announced a third round of quantitative easing, or QE3. Pointing to slow economic growth and an unemployment rate that has not improved since the beginning of the year, the Fed expressed concern that "without further policy accommodation, economic growth might not be strong enough to generate sustained improvement in labor market conditions."[65] QE3 will increase policy accommodation by purchasing additional agency mortgaged-backed securities at a pace of $40 billion per month, which together with its "maturity extension program" to increase the average maturity of its asset holdings as announced in June, will increase the Fed's holdings of long-term assets by about $85 billion per month through the end of 2012. Moreover, in a significant change from the earlier rounds of quantitative easing, the QE3 mortgage-backed security purchases are open-ended, meaning that the Fed is committing to continuing the program until labor market conditions improve. The Fed also gave further "forward guidance" by announcing that it intends to keep the federal funds interest rates at "exceptionally low levels" through mid-2015. On March 20, 2013, the Fed announced it continues to be committed to QE3.[66]

Evaluating the Case for Monetary Stimulus

The Fed's recent policy initiatives to provide successive rounds of monetary stimulus have been criticized. One concern is an increased risk of inflation. Such a large increase in bank reserves could also lead to a rapid increase in the overall money supply through the "money multiplier" effect, which in normal times might generate inflation. At present, the sizable degree of slack in the economy and banks' heightened tendency to hold reserves rather than lend them out keeps the risk of inflation low.

As noted above, one of the reasons for initiating a second round of monetary stimulus in late 2010 was to counter an incipient deflation problem, which is accomplished by policies that exert upward pressure on the level of prices, that is, policies that generate some degree of inflation. The Fed's second round of monetary stimulus seems to have reduced the deflation risk.

Also, some of the recent increase in broad measures of inflation, such as the consumer price index (CPI), is due to the sharp rise in oil and other commodity prices in the first half of 2011 and again in early 2012. However, such inflation effects are most often temporary and not a source of persistent inflationary pressure. The "core CPI," a measure of inflation that does not include volatile food and energy prices, has remained low. Other indicators also suggest that inflation is likely to remain subdued. First, wages, which are generally the most important determinant of unit production costs, have been stable. Second, longer-term inflationary expectations, as measured by the yields on long-term securities, have not risen appreciably.

However, when the economy returns to more normal conditions, reserves would likely need to be removed to avoid excessive upward pressure on prices. The likely unprecedented scale of the reserves that might need to be drained from the economy has raised concerns about whether the Fed could effectively provide the degree of restraint needed to keep inflation under control.

A second criticism of the Fed's monetary stimulus during the recovery is that it is depreciating the dollar. Although influencing the exchange rate is not a stated goal of the Fed's policy, standard macroeconomic theory would predict, all else equal, that a by-product of monetary stimulus would be a depreciation of the dollar (assuming other countries do not similarly alter their monetary policy in response). A weaker dollar would add to the stimulative effect of monetary stimulus on total spending in the United States by increasing exports and decreasing imports. However, countries such as Germany, Japan, and China that have relied on net exports to propel their economic growth are resistant to a depreciating dollar and have criticized the Fed's actions.

As it turns out, the dollar depreciation that has occurred over the last year is, arguably, not the result of Fed actions, but a correction from the appreciation of the dollar in late 2008 and 2009 that was caused by a flight to safety by foreign investors during the financial crisis. At that time, a strong global demand for relatively safe U.S. Treasury securities bid up the dollar's exchange rate. As financial panic receded, the demand for safety abated, and the dollar depreciated to its pre-crisis level.

A third criticism is that monetary stimulus will have little impact on real economic activity. In the current economic environment, with badly weakened household and business balance sheets placing a premium on improving liquidity, it is difficult for monetary policy to get "traction," stimulating the broader economy by pumping reserves into the banking system. For this reason, the stimulus to the real economy from the Fed's successive rounds of quantitative easing have not been expected to be a "cure-all" for sustaining economic recovery. Moreover, how effective monetary stimulus has been is difficult to judge because there is no ready "counterfactual" state of the economy from which to judge its impact on output and employment. Nevertheless, estimates are possible. Using statistical economic models that incorporate past relations between financial conditions and the economy, it is possible to estimate the impact of monetary stimulus on the economy. For example, one recent study found that the first two rounds of quantitative easing may have increased output by 3% and increased employment by more than 2 million jobs.[67] Other studies have found comparable effects.[68]

A Lesson from the Great Depression

One of the important lessons from the Great Depression is to avoid a hasty withdrawal of fiscal and monetary stimulus in a fragile economy still recovering from a sharp economic decline. Beginning in 1933, the U.S. economy rebounded from its sharp fall into what has become known as the Great Depression. From 1933 to 1936, supported by expansionary fiscal and monetary policies, the U.S. economy grew briskly at an average rate of 9.0% and unemployment fell from 25% to 14%. Economic output had nearly returned to its level in 1929, but the economy was still well short of full recovery. But in 1937, the recovery halted and the economy tipped into a second recession. Most economists believe that the second dip into recession was caused by an unfortunate premature switch to contractionary monetary and fiscal policies in a still-fragile recovering economy.

On the monetary side, in 1936, the Federal Reserve began to worry about inflation. After several years of relatively loose monetary policy, the U.S. banking system had built up large quantities of reserves in excess of legal reserve requirements. The Fed feared, despite little overt evidence of a problem, that should the banks begin to lend these excess reserves, it could lead to an overexpansion of credit and generate an inflationary surge. In an attempt to sop up those excess reserves, the Fed raised the banks' reserve requirements three times during 1936. However, banks were still nervous about the financial panics of the early 1930s and uncertain about the durability of the economic recovery, and consequently wanted to hold excess reserves as a cushion. In response to the higher reserve requirements erasing that cushion, the banks worked to rebuild it by reducing lending, leading to a contraction of credit-supported spending.

On the fiscal side, by 1936, following several years of large budget deficits, the federal government had a strong urge to declare victory and get back to normal policy—specifically, balancing the government budget. The veterans' bonus that was paid in 1936 was not renewed in 1937; in addition, Social Security taxes were collected for the first time in 1937. The overall effect was a fiscal contraction equal to about 3% of GDP.

The double hit of contractionary monetary and fiscal policy in an economy that had still not reached the point in which private demand was capable of fully sustaining economic growth led to a recession. In 1938, GDP fell 4.5% and the unemployment rate increased to 19%.[69]

Economic policy quickly changed course and recovery resumed in the second half of 1938, but the policy error added about two years to the Great Depression, which ended with the step-up in war-time government spending in 1941.

The euro zone countries appear to be re-learning this policy lesson from the Great Depression, at considerable economic cost. The IMF's has recently argued that attempts to impose austerity measures to combat growing government debt, while still in the mist of economic recovery, is pulling growth down.[70]

Economic Projections

Given the unusually large deterioration of the balance sheets of households and businesses, the possible reduction of the U.S. economy's level of potential output, the fragile state of the global economy, and uncertainty about fiscal policy, projections of the U.S. economy's near-term path carry a higher than normal degree of uncertainty. During 2012, most economic forecasters have steadily trimmed their growth projections as it became ever more evident that the economy seemed to be only "treading water," particularity in labor markets. Despite "headwinds" from a return to recession in Europe and federal fiscal tightening at home, most forecasters expect the U.S. economic recovery to continue, albeit at a slow pace.

- In its March 2013 meeting, the Fed's Open Market Committee projected real GDP in 2013 to advance in a range between 2.3% and 2.8% and in 2014 advance in a range between 2.9% to 3.4%. The unemployment rate in 2013 is projected to be in a range of 7.3% to 7.5% and in 2014 in a range of 6.5% to 3.5%.[71]
- The IMF's April 2013 projection sees real GDP in the United States increasing 1.9% in 2013 and 3.0% in 2014. Globally, the IMF expects an unbalanced recovery to persist, with growth in the advanced economies in 2013 averaging 3.3% compared with growth in the emerging developing economies in 2013 averaging 5.3%.[72]
- In its February 2013 projection, CBO sees real GDP advancing 1.4% in 2013 and 2.6% in 2014, and the unemployment rate at 7.9% in 2013 and 7.8% in 2014.[73]

End Notes

[1] See CRS Report R40007, Financial Market Turmoil and U.S. Macroeconomic Performance, by Craig K. Elwell.

[2] Real GDP is the total output, adjusted for inflation, of goods and services produced in the United States in a given year.

[3] Data on real GDP are available from the Department of Commerce, Bureau of Economic Analysis, at http://www.bea.gov/national/index.htm#gdp. Size of output gap is based on CRS calculations using Congressional Budget Office estimate of potential GDP, data for which is available at FRED Economic Data, St. Louis Fed, at http://research.stlouisfed.org /fred2/series/GDPPOT.

[4] Data on unemployment and employment are available from the Department of Labor, Bureau of Labor Statistics, at http://www.bls.gov/.

[5] Data on wealth and financial flows available at the Board of Governors of the Federal Reserve System, at http://www.federalreserve.gov/releases/z1/Current/z1r-5.pdf.

[6] See IMF, World Economic Outlook, October 2009, Chapter 2, at http://www.imf.org/external /pubs/ft/weo/2009/02/ pdf/c2.pdf; Ben J. Bernanke, Semiannual Monetary Policy Report to Congress, before the senate Banking Committee, July 21,2010, http://www.federalreserve. gov/newsevents/testimony/bernanke20100721a.htm; and Alan S. Blinder, After the Music Stopped: The Financial Crisis, The Response, and The Work Ahead, Penguin Press, January 24, 2013, Chapter 8.

[7] Agency debt and securities are issued by "government sponsored enterprises" (GSEs), such as Fannie Mae and Freddie Mac.

[8] For further discussion of Fed actions in this period, see CRS Report RL34427, Financial Turmoil: Federal Reserve Policy Responses, by Marc Labonte.

[9] See CRS Report R40104, Economic Stimulus: Issues and Policies, by Jane G. Gravelle, Thomas L. Hungerford, and Marc Labonte.

[10] For more information on TARP, see CRS Report R41427, Troubled Asset Relief Program (TARP): Implementation and Status, by Baird Webel.

[11] The output gap is a measure of the difference between actual output and the output the economy could produce if at full employment.

[12] U.S. Department of Commerce, Bureau of Economic Analysis, National Income and Product Accounts, at http://www.bea.gov/iTable/index_nipa.cfm.

[13] Board of Governors of the Federal Reserve System, Senior Loan Officers Survey on Bank Lending Practices, January 2013, at http://www.federalreserve.gov/boarddocs/SnLoan Survey/.

[14] Spread of 600 basis points is 6%. Data on spreads found at http://www.bloomberg.com/apps /quote?ticker= .TEDSP%3AIND.

[15] Board of Governors of the Federal Reserve System, Statistical Release G.17, March 2013, at http://www.federalreserve.gov/releases/g17/.

[16] Bureau of Labor Statistics, Labor Force Statistics from the Current Population Survey, March 2013, at http://www.bls.gov/cps/.

[17] U.S Census Bureau, New Residential Construction In February2013, joint release, March 19, 2013, at http://www.census.gov/construction/nrc/pdf/newresconst.pdf and S&P Case–Shiller 20-City Home Price Index, available at http://www.standardandpoors.com/indices /sp-case-shiller-home-price-indices/en/us/?indexId=spusacashpidff—p-us.

[18] CRS calculation from Bureau of Economic analysis data for real GDP and CBO estimate of potential GDP both available from Federal Reserve Economic Data (FRED), St. Louis Federal Reserve Bank, at http://research.stlouisfed.org/fred2/.

[19] Bureau of Labor Statistics, Labor Force Statistics from the Current Population Survey, March 2013, http://www.bls.gov/cps/.

[20] See Atif Miam and Amir Sufi, Consumers and the Economy, Part II: Household Debt and the Weak Recovery, Federal Reserve Bank of San Francisco Economic Letter, January 18, 2011.

[21] International Monetary Fund (IMF), World Economic Outlook, January 2013, at http://www.imf.org/external/pubs/ft/ weo/2013/update/01/index.htm.

[22] U.S. Department of Commerce, Bureau of Economic Analysis, National Income and Product Accounts, at http://www.bea.gov/iTable/index_nipa.cfm.

[23] Department of Commerce, Bureau of Economic Analysis, at http://www.bea.gov/national /index.htm#gdp.

[24] The long-term growth of aggregate supply is determined by the growth in the supplies of capital and labor and on the growth in production technology used to turn capital and labor into goods and services.

[25] The Congressional Budget Office, The Budget and Economic Outlook: Fiscal Years 2012 to 2020, January 2012, at http://www.cbo.gov/publication/42905.

[26] Board of Governors of the Federal Reserve System, "Flow of Funds Accounts," Table B.100, March 7, 2013, at http://www.federalreserve.gov/releases/z1/Current/.

[27] See Evan Tanner and Yassar Abdih, "Rebuilding U.S. Wealth," Finance & Development, IMF, December 2009 at http://www.imf.org/external/pubs/ft/fandd/2009/12/tanner.htm.

[28] Board of Governors of the Federal Reserve System, "Flow of Funds Accounts," Table B.100, March 7, 2013, at http://www.federalreserve.gov/releases/z1/Current/z1r-5.pdf.

[29] Board of Governors of the Federal Reserve System, "Flow of Funds Accounts," Table B.100, March 7, 2013, at http://www.federalreserve.gov/releases/z1/Current/z1r-5.pdf.

[30] The standard model of consumer spending used in economic analysis assumes that consumers seek to avoid large swings in their living standards over the course of their lifetimes. Thus as incomes rise and fall both in the short and long term, individuals are expected to vary their saving rate in order to minimize the effect on their consumption. If consumers seek to

maintain a fairly stable level of consumption over their entire lives, then the level of consumption at any given point in their lives will depend on their current wealth and some expectation about their income over the rest of their lives. See Annamaria Lusardi, Jonathan Skinner, and Steven Venti, "Saving Puzzles and Saving Policies in the United States," National Bureau of Economic Research, Working Paper 8237, April 2001.

[31] See CRS Report R40647, The Fall and Rise of Household Saving, by Brian W. Cashell.

[32] U.S. Department of Commerce, Bureau of Economic Analysis, National Income and Product Accounts, Table 5.1, http://www.bea.gov/national/nipaweb/SelectTable.asp?Selected=N.

[33] U.S. Energy Information Administration, Petroleum; Weekly Spot Price, July 2012, at http://www.eia.gov/dnav/pet/ hist/LeafHandler.ashx?n=PET&s=RCLC1&f=D.

[34] Research indicates that a $10 increase in the per barrel price of oil sustained for two years is likely to reduce real GDP growth relative to base-line by 0.2 percentage points in the first year and 0.5 percentage points in the second year. See U.S. Energy Information Administration, Economic Effects of High Oil Prices, 2006, http://www.eia.gov/oiaf/aeo/ otheranalysis/aeo_2006analysispapers/efhop.html.

[35] Ibid., Table 1.1.5.

[36] Department of Commerce, Bureau of Economic Analysis, National Income and Product Accounts, Table 1.1.5, athttp://www.bea.gov/national/index.htm#gdp.

[37] Ibid., Table 1.1.5, at http://www.bea.gov/national/index.htm#gdp.

[38] U.S. Census Bureau, Housing Vacancies and Home Ownership, at http://www.census.gov/hhes /www/housing/hvs/ historic/.

[39] Data for capacity utilization are available at Board of Governors of the Federal Reserve System, Industrial Production and Capacity Utilization, Table G17, http://www.federal reserve.gov/releases/g17/.

[40] Bureau of Economic Analysis, National Income and Product Accounts, Table 1.1.5, at http://www.bea.gov/national/ index.htm#gdp.

[41] Department of Commerce, Bureau of Economic Analysis, National Income and Product Accounts, Table 1.1.6, at http://www.bea.gov/iTable/iTable.cfm?ReqID=9&step=1.

[42] On global rebalancing, see for example, Olivier Blanchard, "Sustaining Global Recovery," International Monetary Fund, September 2009, "Rebalancing," The Economist, March 31, 2010, at http://www.imf.org/external/pubs/ft/fandd/ 2009/09/index.htm, and Board of Governors of the Federal Reserve System, Vice-chairman Donald L. Kohn, Speech "Global Imbalances," May 11, 2010, at http://www.federalreserve.gov/newsevents/speech/kohn 20100511a.htm.

[43] OECD, Restoring Public Finances, Country Notes: Germany, 2010, at http://www.oecd.org /gov/ budgetingandpublicexpenditures/47840777.pdf.

[44] Of course, for these reforms to translate into a shift in China's trade balance, that nation must be willing to allow its' exchange rate to rise relative to the dollar, causing a decrease in the price of foreign goods relative to domestic goods, and exerting downward pressure on China's trade surplus. From July 2005 to February 2009, China abandoned its dollar peg, allowing the yuan to appreciate by 28% (on a real trade-weighted basis). However, faced with weakening export sales due to the global financial crisis China for the last 10 months has re-pegged the yuan to the dollar. China's export-led growth model, relying on a high saving rate (to keep internal demand low) and a low exchange rate pegged to the dollar (to keep external demand high), has been very successful and, despite the possible advantages of reforms to boost domestic demand, it is uncertain whether China would move substantially away from this model.

[45] The Congressional Budget Office, Key Assumptions in Projecting Potential Output, August 2012, at http://www.cbo.gov/publication/43541.

[46] P. Kannan, A. Scott, and M. Terrones, "From Recession to Recovery: How Soon and How Strong?," in World Economic Outlook, International Monetary Fund, April 2009, pp. 103-138. Also see Davide Furceri and Annabelle Mourougane, The Effect of Financial Crisis on Potential Output: New Empirical Evidence from OECD Countries, OECD Economics Department, Working Paper no. 699, May 2009.

[47] Employment in construction, financial services, and some types of manufacturing may remain depressed for some time, requiring some who lose their jobs in those sectors to seek employment in other sectors. See also CRS Report R41785, The Increase in Unemployment Since 2007: Is It Cyclical or Structural?, by Linda Levine, which suggests that most of current U.S. unemployment is cyclical.

[48] Department of Commerce, Bureau of Economic Analysis, National Income and Product Accounts, Table 1.1.6, at http://www.bea.gov/iTable/iTable.cfm?ReqID=9&step=1.

[49] The Congressional Budget Office, Budget and Economic Outlook: An Update, August 2012, Table 2-3, at http://www.cbo.gov/doc.cfm?index=12316.

[50] Lawrence H. Summers, "Reflections on Fiscal Policy and Economic Strategy," Speech at the Johns Hopkins School of Advanced International Studies, May 24, 2010, at http://www.whitehouse.gov/administration/eop/nec/speeches/ fiscal-policy-economic-strategy. Other economists have also concluded that further stimulus is called for. See, for example, Brad DeLong "The Worst -of-Both-Worlds Fiscal Policy," June 18, 2010, http://delong.typepad.com/sdj/ 2010/06/worst-of-both-worlds-fiscal-policy.html; and "The Case for More Stimulus" Interview with William Gale of the Brookings Institution, June 2010, at http://www.theatlantic.com/business/archive/2010/06/the-case-for-morestimulus /57776/.

[51] The Congressional Budget Office, CBO Estimate of Changes in Revenue and Direct Spending for the Tax Relief, Unemployment Insurance Reauthorization, and Job Creation Act of 2010, at http://www.cbo.gov/ftpdocs/120xx/ doc12020/sa4753.pdf.

[52] Department of Commerce, Bureau of Economic Analysis, National Income and Product Accounts, Tables 1.1.1 and 1.1.2, at http://www.bea.gov/iTable/iTable.cfm?Req ID=9&step=1.

[53] The Congressional Budget Office, The Budget and Economic Outlook:Fiscal Years2013 to 2023, February 5, 2013, available at http://www.cbo.gov/publication/43907.

[54] See for example, Derek Thompson, "The Case Against More Stimulus," The Atlantic, June 2010, at http://www.theatlantic.com/business/archive/2010/06/the-case-against-more-stimulus/57774/, and "Here's Why Fiscal Stimulus Won't Work," The Atlantic, February 2010, at http://www.theatlantic.com/business/archive/2010/02/hereswhy-government-stimulus-does-not-work/36466/.

[55] This theory is called "Ricardian equivalence." It is named after the nineteenth-century economist David Ricardo who first made the argument. For further discussion see N. Gregory Mankiw, Principles of Economics (Ft. Worth, Dryden Press, 1998), p. 556, and Robert J. Barro, "Are Government Bonds Net Wealth?" Journal of Political Economy, vol. 82, no. 6 (November-December, 1974), pp. 1095-1117.

[56] See CRS Report RL31235, The Economics of the Federal Budget Deficit, by Brian W. Cashell; Alan J. Auerbach and William G. Gale, "Activist Fiscal Policy to Stabilize Economic Activity," working paper, September 29, 2009, available at http://elsa.berkeley.edu/~auerbach/activistfiscal.pdf; and Robert E. Hall, "By How Much Does GDP Rise If the Government Buys More Output?" Brookings Papers on Economic

Activity, fall 2009, pp. 183- 250. On the probable simulative impact of alternative fiscal measures see CBO, Policies for Increasing Economic Growth and Employment, March 2010, at http://www.cbo.gov/ftpdocs/112xx/doc11255/02-23-Employment_Testimony.pdf, and J. Bradford DeLong and Lawrence H. Summers, "Fiscal Policy in a Depressed Economy," The Brookings Institution, March 2012.

[57] For discussion of the long-term debt issue, see President Obama's National Commission on Fiscal Responsibility and Reform, at http://www.fiscalcommission.gov/.

[58] For further discussion of this issue, see CRS Report R41849, Can Contractionary Fiscal Policy Be Expansionary?, by Jane G. Gravelle and Thomas L. Hungerford.

[59] For more information on the BCA, see CRS Report R41965, The Budget Control Act of 2011, by Bill Heniff Jr., Elizabeth Rybicki, and Shannon M. Mahan; and the Congressional Budget Office, Budget and Economic Outlook: An Update, August 2011, p. 38, at http://www.cbo.gov/doc.cfm?index=12316.

[60] On the policy of quantitative easing, see CRS Report R41540, Quantitative Easing and the Growth in the Federal Reserve's Balance Sheet, by Marc Labonte; and CRS Report RL30354, Monetary Policy and the Federal Reserve: Current Policy and Conditions, by Marc Labonte.

[61] Board of Governors of the Federal Reserve System, Federal Open Market Committee, http://www.federalreserve.gov/ monetarypolicy/fomccalendars.htm.

[62] For further discussion of deflation, see CRS Report R40512, Deflation: Economic Significance, Current Risk, and Policy Responses, by Craig K. Elwell.

[63] Board of Governors of the Federal Reserve System, press release, September 2011, at http://www.federalreserve.gov/ newsevents/press/monetary/20110921a.htm.

[64] Board of Governors of the Federal Reserve System, press release, June 2012, at http://www.federalreserve.gov/ newsevents/press/monetary/20120620a.htm.

[65] Board of Governors of the Federal Reserve System, press release, September 13, 2012, at http://www.federalreserve.gov/newsevents/press/monetary/20120913a.htm.

[66] Board of Governors of the Federal Reserve System, press release, March 20, 2013, at http://www.federalreserve.gov/ newsevents/press/monetary/20130320a.htm.

[67] Hess Chung, Jean-Phillippe Laforte, David Reifschender, and John C. Williams, "Have We Underestimated the Likelihood and Severity of Zero Lower Bound Events," Journal of Money, Credit and Banking, vol. 44, issue si (February 2012), pp. 47-82.

[68] See for example, Jeffrey C. Fuher and Giovanni P. Olivei, "The Estimated Macroeconomic Effects of the Federal Reserve's Large-Scale Treasury Purchase Program," Public Policy Briefs, April 2011, Federal Reserve Bank of Boston; and Michael Kiley "The Aggregate Demand Effects of Short-Term and Long-Term Interest Rates," Finance and Economics Discussion Series 2012-54, Board of Governors of the Federal Reserve System, Washington DC.

[69] For further discussion of the recession of 1937, see Christina D. Romer, "The Nation in Depression," Journal of Economic Perspectives 7 (spring 1993), pp. 19-39; Milton Friedman and Anna D. Schwartz, A Monetary History of the United States, 1867-1960 (Princeton, NJ: Princeton University Press, 1963); Francois R. Velde, "The Recession of 1937—A Cautionary Tale," Economic Perspectives, Federal Reserve Bank of Chicago, fourth quarter 2009, pp. 16-36.

[70] See remarks by Olivier Blanchard in the International Monetary Fund, World Economic Outlook, October 2012, Forward, at http://www.imf.org/external/pubs/ft/weo/2012/02 /index.htm.

[71] Board of Governors of the Federal Reserve System, Minutes of March 12 FOMC Meeting, Projection Materials, at http://www.federalreserve.gov/monetarypolicy/fomccalendars.htm.

[72] International Monetary Fund, World Economic Outlook, April 2013, Table 1.1, http://www.imf.org/external/pubs/ft/weo/2013/01/pdf/text.pdf.

[73] CBO Budget and Economic Outlook, February 2013, at http://www.cbo.gov/publication /43907.

In: After the Financial Crisis
Editor: Edgar I. Bair
ISBN: 978-1-62948-593-5

Chapter 3

REBUILDING HOUSEHOLD WEALTH: IMPLICATIONS FOR ECONOMIC RECOVERY*

Craig K. Elwell

SUMMARY

The pace of economic recovery from the 2007-2009 recession has been historically slow. Over four years of recovery, the annual rate of growth of real gross domestic product (GDP) has averaged 2%, well below the 3% to 5% typical of other post-WWII recoveries. As a result, the output gap—the difference between what the economy could produce and what it actually produced—has only declined from a high of 8.1% in mid-2009 to a still large 5.8% in mid- 2013. Slow growth of output has translated into a slow reduction of unemployment.

The recovery has persisted, in part, due to support to aggregate spending by policies of fiscal and monetary stimulus. However, fiscal stimulus has steadily dissipated since 2010 and in 2013 the federal budget has turned contractionary. While monetary policy is expected to remain stimulative through 2013, it is unlikely to add to that stimulus to counteract the increasing drag of falling federal budget deficits on economic activity. Therefore, sustaining the recovery's momentum in the remainder of 2013 and into 2014 may require a greater push from private spending, particularly household consumption spending.

---

* This is an edited, reformatted and augmented version of Congressional Research Service, Publication No. R43228, dated September 13, 2013.

In the aftermath of the 2007-2009 recession, which involved a substantial loss of net worth and increase in the burden of debt, households' actions to repair their severely damaged balance sheets by reducing debt and building wealth is thought by many economists to be a key factor dissipating the strength of consumer spending. Although this repair is necessary for building a stronger economy in the long run, it has slowed the economy-wide recovery and job creation in the short run.

Where households currently stand in repairing their balance sheets is likely to influence the strength of consumer spending going forward. If substantially complete, it would point to the prospect of stronger consumer spending and increased momentum of the economic recovery; but if substantial wealth building is still needed, it would diminish that prospect.

A number of indicators paint a mixed picture of the prospect for stronger consumer spending. Despite clear progress, more repair of the severely damaged household balance sheet may be needed before households begin to spend at a faster pace. The typical household has likely only seen modest improvement in its net worth in large measure because the value of real estate, most often the largest asset it holds, has only recently been increasing. The rebound of the housing market portends progress for the typical household rebuilding its wealth, but it is unlikely that this process will be completed in 2013, making it also likely that tepid spending by consumers will continue.

Determining the state of household net worth has implications for the optimal policy response going forward. If household net worth is judged to have not fully recovered from the damage incurred in 2007-2009, particularly for the typical household, some may regard this as an indicator of a continuing need for macroeconomic policy to provide stimulus to maintain the recovery's upward momentum. It could also have implications for federal policy measures that are aimed at providing direct help in removing the burden of household debt through programs that restructure mortgage debt.

INTRODUCTION

Congress was an active participant in the policy responses to the 2007-2009 recession and its aftermath and has an ongoing interest in macroeconomic conditions. Current macroeconomic concerns include whether the economy is in a sustained recovery, rapidly reducing unemployment, and speeding a return to normal output and employment growth.

Faced with fiscal consolidation and limited further impetus from monetary policy, the momentum of the current economic recovery will likely be determined by the strength of spending by the private economy, particularly the strength of consumer spending. In the aftermath of the deep 2007-2009 recession, involving a huge loss of net worth and a large increase in the burden of debt, households' actions to repair their balance sheets is thought by many economists to be a key factor dissipating the strength of consumer spending and, in turn, slowing economy-wide recovery and job creation. Where households currently stand in repairing their balance sheets is likely to have a strong effect on the strength of consumer spending. If substantially complete, it would point to the prospect of stronger consumer spending and increased momentum of the economic recovery; but if substantial wealth building is still needed, it would diminish that prospect.

This report begins with a discussion (accompanied by graphics) of the slower than normal pace of the ongoing economic recovery and the likely role in that of weak consumer spending forced by a sharp loss of household net worth during the recession and the subsequent need to rebuild that lost wealth. Next, the report examines (also accompanied by graphics) where balance sheet repair currently stands, paying particular attention to the composition of assets that have been accumulated and the degree of debt reduction achieved. The report then considers the near-term prospect for stronger consumer spending and more rapid economic recovery. The report concludes with a discussion of the possible implications of household balance sheet repair for economic policy.

BACKGROUND: HOUSEHOLD WEALTH AND ECONOMIC ACTIVITY

A Deep Recession and a Slower Than Normal Recovery

The 2007-2009 recession was long and deep, and according to several indicators was the most severe economic contraction since the 1930s (but nevertheless much less severe than the Great Depression). When the fall of economic activity finally bottomed out in the second half of 2009, real gross domestic product (GDP) had contracted by approximately 5.1%, or by about $680 billion.

The pace of economic recovery from the recession has been lackluster.[1] Over four years of recovery, the annual rate of growth of real GDP has averaged 2%, well below the 3% to 5% typical of other post-WWII recoveries.

As a result, the output gap—the difference between what the economy could produce and what it actually produced—has only declined from a high of 8.1% in mid-2009 to a still large 5.8% in mid- 2013 (see **Figure 1**). Slow growth of output has also meant a slow reduction of unemployment; down from a peak of 10.1% reached in October 2009, the unemployment rate remains near 7.5%, leaving 12 million persons still without a job.[2]

Albeit slower than hoped, the recovery has persisted. In part, steady growth was the result of support given to aggregate spending by policies of fiscal and monetary stimulus. However, fiscal stimulus has steadily dissipated since 2010 and in 2013 it has turned contractionary.[3] And while monetary policy is expected to remain stimulative through 2013, it is unlikely to add to that stimulus to counteract increasing fiscal drag. Therefore, sustaining the recovery's momentum in the remainder of 2013 and into 2014 may require a greater push from private spending, particularly household consumption spending.

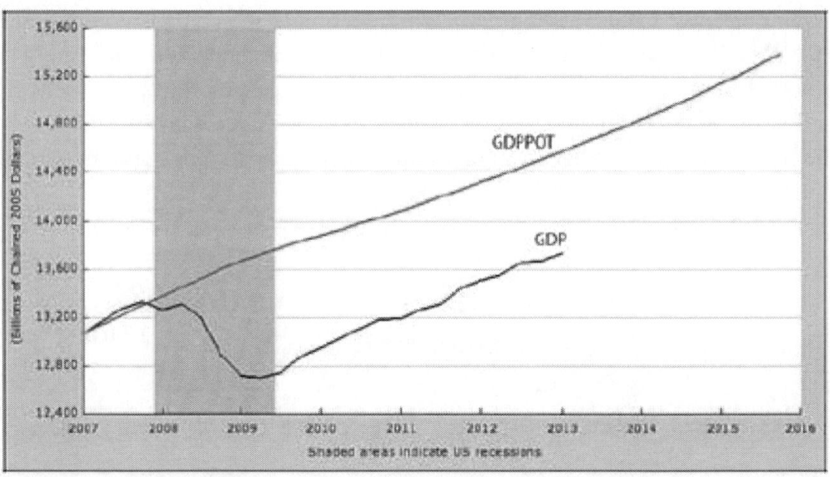

Sources: Congressional Budget Office and Bureau of Economic Analysis.

Figure 1. Potential GDP (GDPPOT),Actual GDP, and the Output Gap.

Unusually Weak Consumption Spending

Personal consumption expenditures historically constitute the largest and most stable component of aggregate spending in the U.S. economy. Since the 1980s, consumption spending's share of GDP has averaged between 65% and

70% and during previous post-war recoveries consumption spending has typically increased at a 4%-5% annual pace. Typically, a strong rebound by the largest component of final demand was a central driver sustaining the momentum of economic recovery, causing a quick closing of the output gap opened up by the preceding recession, and a quick return to full employment. This recovery, however, has been characterized by relatively weak consumption spending by households, averaging a sluggish 2% annual pace for the four-year period. Several factors have likely contributed to households spending less vigorously in this recovery than in previous economic recoveries. Persistent high rates of unemployment have directly dampened spending by decreasing income for millions of households and more broadly dampened spending by eroding consumers' confidence in their immediate economic prospects. In addition, sharp spikes in energy prices in 2010 and 2012 had significant negative effects on household budgets.[4]

The Impact of a Large Decrease in Household Wealth

Many economists have argued that the most important factor making consumer spending in this recovery historically weak is that, unlike previous post-war recessions in which reduced household income impeded spending, the 2007-2009 recession carried with it an enormous decrease in household net worth (wealth) caused by the associated collapse of the housing and stock markets. The $542 billion or 5.3% decrease in disposable income during the recession was large but substantially smaller than the decline in aggregate household wealth, which decreased by $16.4 trillion or 26% (see Figure 2).[5]

However, the loss of wealth for the typical household was proportionately greater than the fall of aggregate household wealth. A clearer view of the damage to the net worth of a typical household is provided by the change in *median* household net worth—the level of net worth at which half the households are richer and half poorer. The estimated decrease in median household real net worth was 39%. Overall, it is estimated that the bottom 80% of households lost two decades' worth of wealth.[6]

Although declines in the values of financial assets or businesses were important factors for some families, owner equity in the home has typically constituted 75%-80% of households' total assets. Therefore, the decrease in the median household's net worth appears to have been driven most strongly by an $8.4 trillion or 35% decrease in the value of real estate assets that began in 2006 and continued through mid-2011 (see Figure 3).[7] The variation in housing wealth is largely explained by changes in home values, rather than changes in home ownership rates, which have remained largely unchanged. A commonly used measure of home prices is the Case-Shiller index, which tracks home prices in 20 metropolitan regions. Over the 2006-2011 period, the Case-Shiller index fell 33% and its path essentially mirrors the path of the value of household real estate assets (see Figure 4).[8]

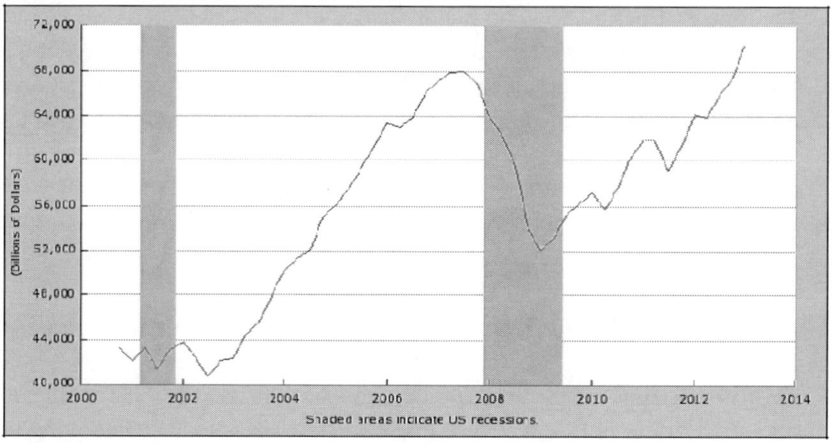

Source: Board of Governors of the Federal Reserve System.

Figure 2. Aggregate Household Net Worth.

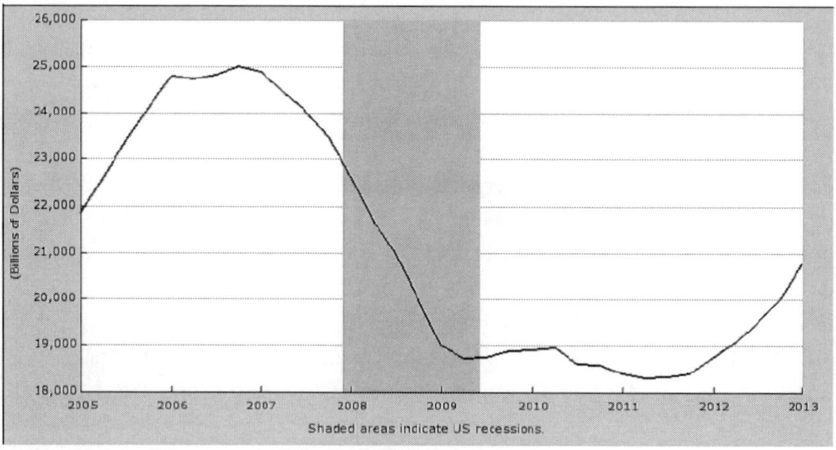

Source: Board of Governors of the Federal Reserve System.

Figure 3. Value of Household Real Estate Assets.

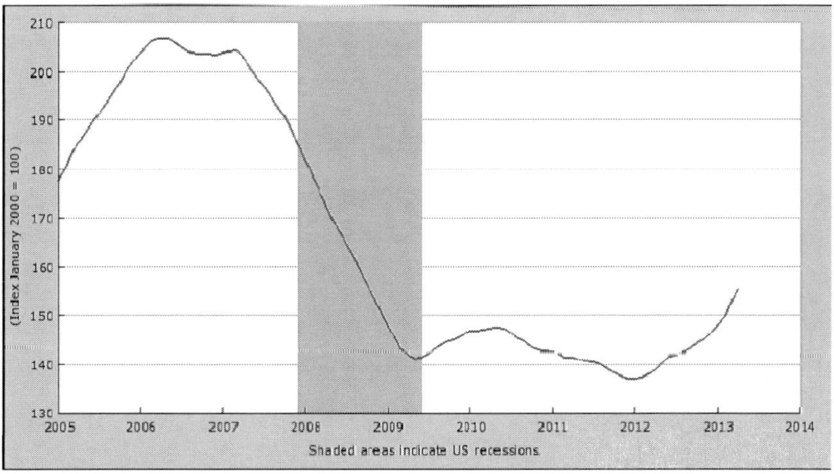

Source: Standard & Poors/Dow Jones.

Figure 4. Case-Shiller Home Price Index.

Research suggests that housing wealth has a much stronger impact on household spending than does financial wealth, making it a major factor governing consumption spending by most households. It is estimated that a one-time decrease in housing wealth of 1% leads to a 0.10% decrease in consumer spending each year afterward. On the other hand, the same change in financial wealth (i.e., stocks, bonds, pension funds) led to a smaller 0.03% permanent decrease in consumer spending. That degree of consumption sensitivity to housing wealth implies that the 35% decrease in housing wealth experienced between 2006 and 2011 would reduce household consumption by 3.5% or by about $350 billion, which is equivalent to more than half of the $680 billion economy-wide contraction of real GDP during the 2007-2009 recession.[9]

The Added Burden on Households of Increased Financial Leverage

The loss of wealth by itself would have likely caused households to divert more income from consumption to saving in an attempt to rebuild their net worth. However, there was another exacerbating factor—a sharp increase in financial leverage. Leverage is the degree to which household assets are financed with debt and is typically measured as the ratio of household debt to assets. In 2007 the leverage ratio of households balance sheet was at a historically high 18%, up from 14% in 2000. With the collapse of asset prices that began in 2006, the leverage ratio would rise, reaching over 21% at the end of the recession in mid-2009 (see Figure 5).

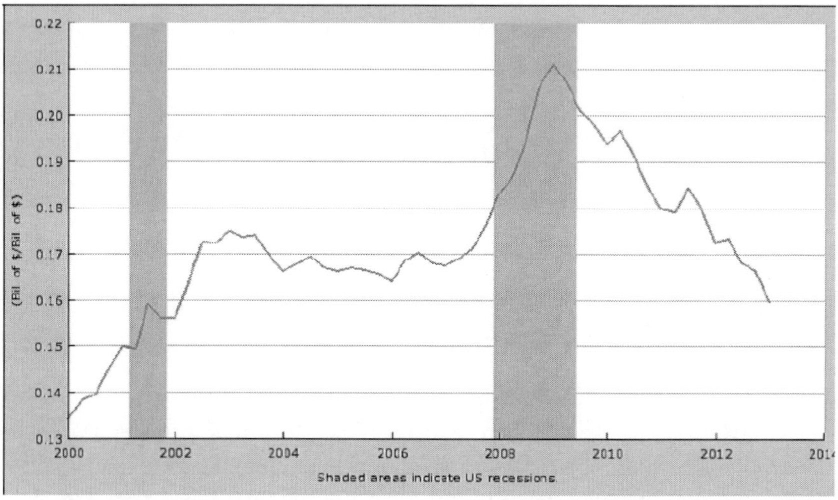

Source: Board of Governors of the Federal Reserve System.

Figure 5. Leverage in the Household Balance Sheet: Ratio of Debt to Assets.

Many analysts argued that this "debt overhang" created an additional motive for household deleveraging, giving rise to a further diversion of current income to balance sheet repair and, in turn, causing slower aggregate spending. Sharply rising debt likely dampens household spending by raising financial discomfort, increasing debt service costs, and reducing access to credit markets. A recent study suggests that highly leveraged households had larger declines in spending than other households, despite having smaller changes in net worth.[10]

Together, a substantial loss of net worth and historically high leverage created a particularly weak aggregate household balance sheet, increasing the severity of the 2007-2009 recession and slowing the pace of the subsequent recovery. Research suggests that roughly two out of every three jobs lost between 2007 and 2009 were attributable to household balance sheet weakness leading to weak consumption spending[11].

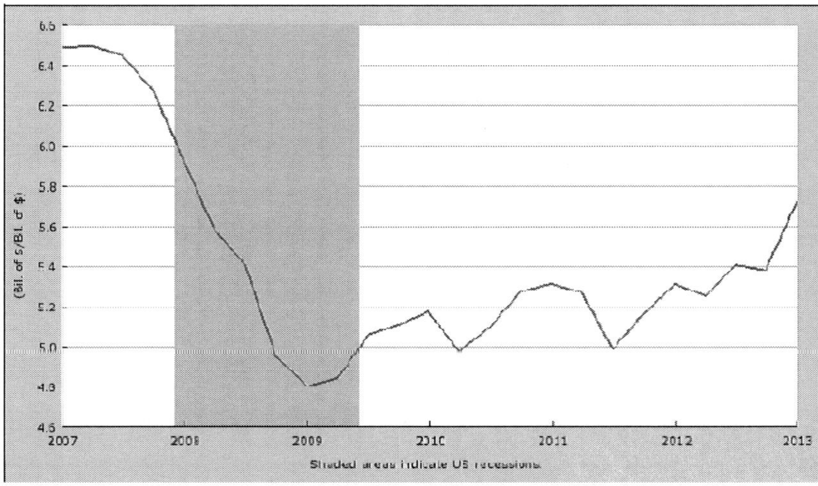

Source : Board of Governors of the Federal Reserve System.

Figure 6. Ratio of Household Net Worth to Disposable Income.

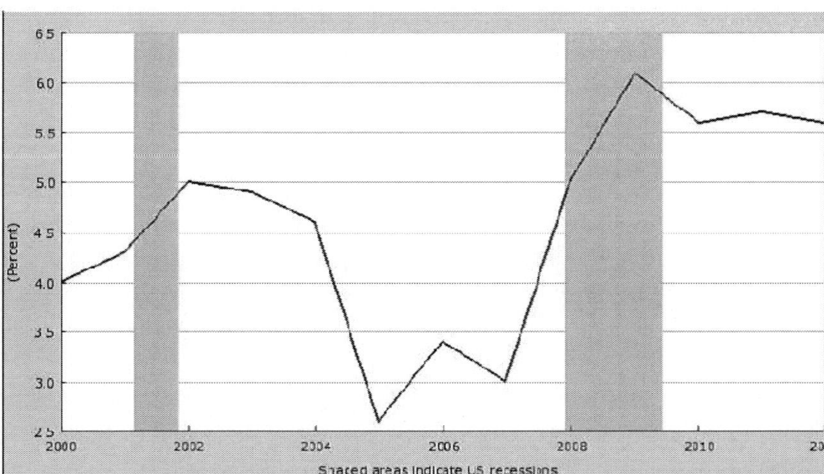

Source: Bureau of Economic Analysis.

Figure 7. Personal Saving Rate.

Similarly, unlike in earlier post-war recoveries, the need for households to rebuild a sizable amount of lost wealth and to reduce a large debt overhang would cause a substantial diversion of current income from consumption spending to saving. The process of repairing the household balance sheet has been, arguably, a major factor causing the below average pace of the economic recovery since 2009.[12] The ratio of net worth to disposable income is one indicator that households have been repairing their balance sheets; it has been increasing, moving from a recession low of 4.5 to 5.9 in the first quarter of 2013 (see Figure 6).[13] Since the start of the recession, the personal saving rate also shows that a larger share of income has been directed toward wealth building. Saving rose from about 2% of income prior to the recession to near 6% during the recession, and it has remained above 5% during the recovery (see Figure 7).

The Current State of Household Net Worth

Aggregate Nominal Household Net Worth is Now Above the Pre-Crisis Level

Aggregate household net worth has more than fully recouped the wealth lost during the 2008- 2009 recession. In the first quarter of 2013, aggregate household net worth reached $70.3 trillion, an increase of $18.3 trillion from the $52.0 trillion low reached in the first quarter of 2009, and about $2.0 trillion above the pre-recession peak of $68.1 trillion reached in the second quarter of 2007 (see Figure 2). The increase in household wealth since 2009 was the net effect of a rising value of assets and falling value of liabilities (debt) although the former was by far the largest contributor to the improvement in net worth (see Figure 8). Since the first quarter of 2009, the value of total assets held by households increased by $17.8 trillion, representing about 97% of the increase in net worth, whereas total liabilities fell by $0.5 trillion, representing the remaining 3% of the increase in net worth. However, aggregate net worth does not tell the complete story about the health of the typical household's balance sheet and the likely inducement provided to consumer spending.

The Recovery in *Real* Household Net Worth is Incomplete

Inflation affects the real purchasing power of wealth. Although inflation has been historically low since the beginning of the recession in late 2007, consumer prices, as measured by the Personal Consumption Expenditures

(PCE) price index, have increased at an annual rate near 2%; the cumulative effect has resulted in a decrease in the purchasing power of a dollar of wealth over the 2007-2013 period by 9.6%.[14] Deflating the current value of household net worth by that factor reduces aggregate net worth in the first quarter of 2013 from $70.3 trillion to $64.3 trillion in 2007dollars; placing real net worth about $4.0 trillion or about 6% short of full recovery of the 2007 level of purchasing power.

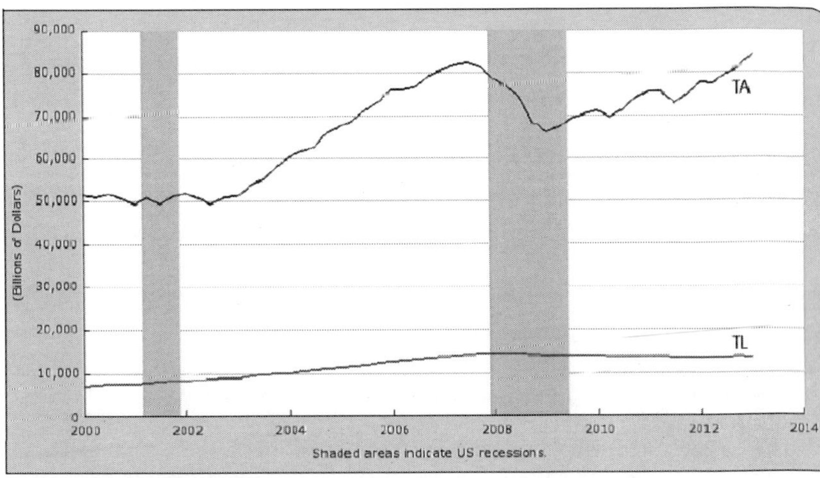

Source: Board of Governors of the Federal Reserve System.

Figure 8. Household's Total Assets (TA) and Liabilities (TL).

Assets with Greatest Increase in Value Since 2009 Are Not Widely Held

The aggregate net worth numbers masks a significant change in the composition of the households underlying assets. On the asset side, the total gain of household net worth was $10.8 trillion. Most (96%) of that gain was highly concentrated in financial assets (i.e., bank deposits, stocks, bonds, pension fund reserves), which increased by $10.4 trillion, and the share of financial assets that comprise total household assets increased from 63% to 69% (see Figure 9). The value of households' nonfinancial assets increased a comparatively modest $2.2 trillion, an increase that was largely the consequence of a like-sized increase in the value of household real estate holdings and is relatively recent, beginning in mid-2011. In addition, non-financial assets share of total household assets has fallen from a pre-crisis share of 35 % to 31% currently.

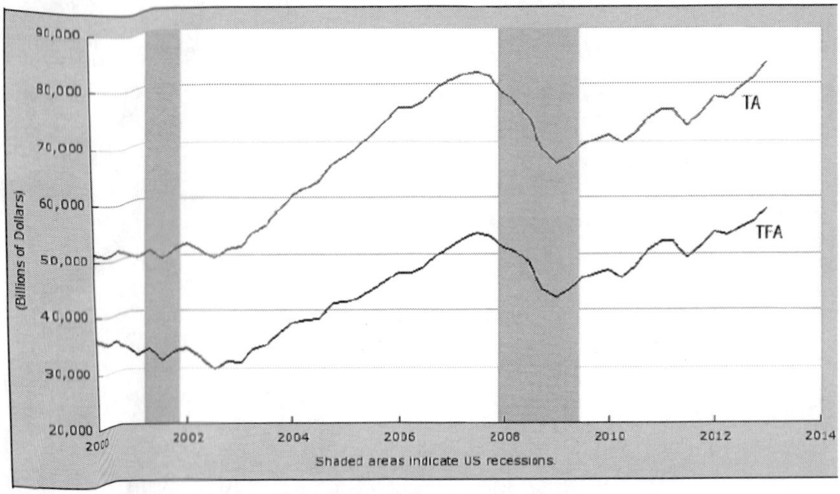

Source: Board of Governors of the Federal Reserve System.

Figure 9. Household's Total Assets (TA) and Financial Assets (TFA).

The possible significance of this shift toward holding more financial assets as a percentage of totals assets is that such assets are not held widely, tending to be concentrated among a relatively small number of wealthier households whose tendency to spend in response to a rise in wealth is likely relatively low. Census data indicates that the real net worth of the median household, at least through 2011, had not increased. Data on the wealth of the median household are only available for select years, the most recent being 2011. In 2005, median household net worth was estimated to be $93,200; at the recessions trough in 2009, it had fallen to $68,900; and remained essentially unchanged in 2011 at $68,800.[15] The lack of improvement in the median household's net worth is largely a reflection of the decline in the value of household real estate holdings; historically a major component of the median household's wealth. Home equity fell by more than $7 trillion from 2006 to 2009 and has only begun to recover since 2012 (see Figure 10), for which median wealth data are not yet available. Consequently, most households have not seen the degree of recovery in their net worth indicated by the aggregate numbers and have a commensurately smaller inducement to boost spending.

Looking at the aggregate home equity data, during much of this period, more than 30% of all mortgages were estimated to be "underwater," meaning that the remaining balance of the mortgage exceeded the value of the home. In the first quarter of 2013, the percentage of underwater mortgages decreased to about 27%, indicating that this important component of net worth has still not fully recovered for an estimated 13 million households, whose ability to spend is likely to be particularly liquidity constrained.[16]

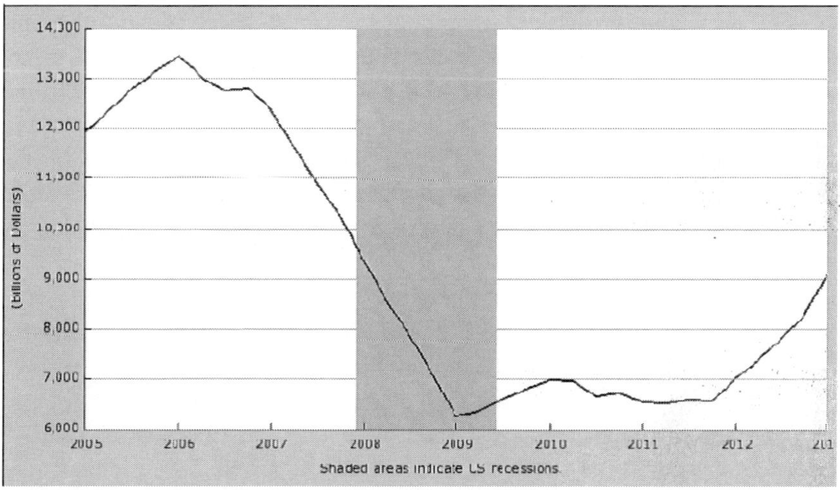

Source: Board of Governors of the Federal Reserve System.

Figure 10. Household's Owner Equity in Real Estate.

Recent Upturn in House Prices Could Boost Typical Household Net Worth

In the second half of 2011, home prices did stabilize and begin to increase, up about 9% on average nationwide through the first quarter of 2013.[17] Rising home prices are likely to have a strong positive effect on the wealth of the median household, and such an improvement is evident in the aggregate net worth data. With house prices once again rising, owner equity in real estate, which had fallen $7.5 trillion from 2006 to 2011, increased $2.6 trillion through the first quarter of 2013 (see Figure 10).

The recent upturn in house prices is likely to have had a positive effect on the net worth of the typical household in 2012 and will continue to do so in

2013 if prices continue rising. Furthermore, dollar for dollar increased housing wealth is likely to have a larger positive effect on household spending relative to increased financial wealth. As also noted above, however, large numbers of mortgage holding households still remain "underwater."

A Modest Reduction in Debt

On the liability side of household's balance sheet, debt obligations decreased from a pre-crisis high of about $14.4 trillion to $13.4 trillion through the first quarter of 2013, reflecting a net decrease of about $1.0 trillion or 7% (see Figure 11). That decline was more than fully explained by a $1.3 trillion decrease in mortgage debt. (Other components of total liabilities, such as consumer credit, increased.) However, these aggregate liability numbers likely overstate changes in active debt repayment behavior by households due to the effect of charge-offs resulting from mortgage defaults that increased greatly between 2007 and 2013. Data limitations prevent a precise allocation of percentages of mortgage debt decline to charge-offs; however, estimates are typically tallied to be several hundreds of billions of dollars.[18]

Households' debt service costs have decreased, down from a high of 14% of disposable income in 2007 to about 10.5% in the first quarter of 2013. However, in addition to a reduced level of debt, a sizable fall in interest rates since 2007 has also lowered debt service costs.[19]

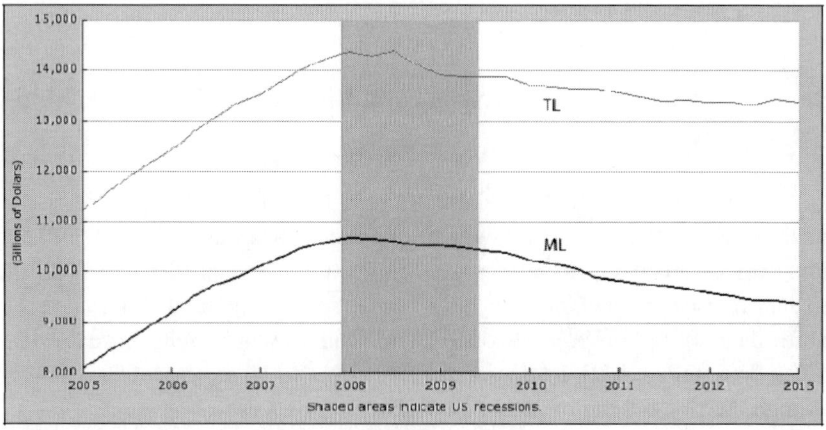

Source: Board of Governors of the Federal Reserve System.

Figure 11. Household's Total Liabilities (TL) and Mortgage Liabilities (ML).

Leverage in the Household Balance Sheet Has Been Reduced

The improvement in the aggregate household balance sheet has also reduced the degree of financial leverage, falling from the recession high of 21% to 16%, which is below the pre-recession leverage ratio value of 17% (See Figure 5). Nevertheless, whether there is still excess leverage or a debt overhang depends on where the current leverage ratio stands relative to where households would prefer to be, but this "desired" leverage is difficult to gauge. A 16% leverage ratio is still historically high. For comparison, from 1970 to 2000 that ratio was consistently below 16%, moving in a band from 12% to 15%.

Perhaps, the typical household may not view a reduction of the aggregate leverage ratio, which largely resulted from the increased value of financial assets with only modest debt reduction, as favorably as the same reduction generated primarily by a sizable increase in housing wealth or a sizable reduction of mortgage debt. There is the possibility that the severity of the financial crisis and the recent precarious state of household finances may have forced a sharp decline in the desired leverage ratio for any given mix of assets on their balance sheet, possibly below the 2006 benchmark.

A leverage ratio that looks more narrowly at the major asset and liability held by the median household, that is, household mortgage debt relative to the market value of household real estate does not show the same degree of improvement as does the broader aggregate leverage ratio. The narrower measure rises from a pre-housing crisis low of 36% in 2006 to a high of 56% in mid-2009, but had fallen to only 45% through the first quarter of 2013 (see Figure 12). By this measure, more deleveraging would be needed to get the ratio back to its 2006 value.

Again, there is the possibility that the severity of the financial crisis and the recent precarious state of household finances may have forced a sharp lowering below the 2006 benchmark of the desired leverage ratio for real estate assets. Prior to the 1990s, this ratio was typically below 30%. One study judged that in 2011, between 20 percent and 25 percent of households were still above their target leverage ratio.[20]

How Much Balance Sheet Repair Has Occurred?

Despite clear progress, more repair of the severely damaged household balance sheet may be needed before households begin to spend at a faster pace. The typical household has likely only seen modest improvement in its net worth (in large measure) because the value of real estate assets has only recently been rising. The rebound of the housing market portends well for the typical household rebuilding its wealth, but it is unlikely that this process will be completed in 2013, making it also likely that tepid spending by consumers will continue.

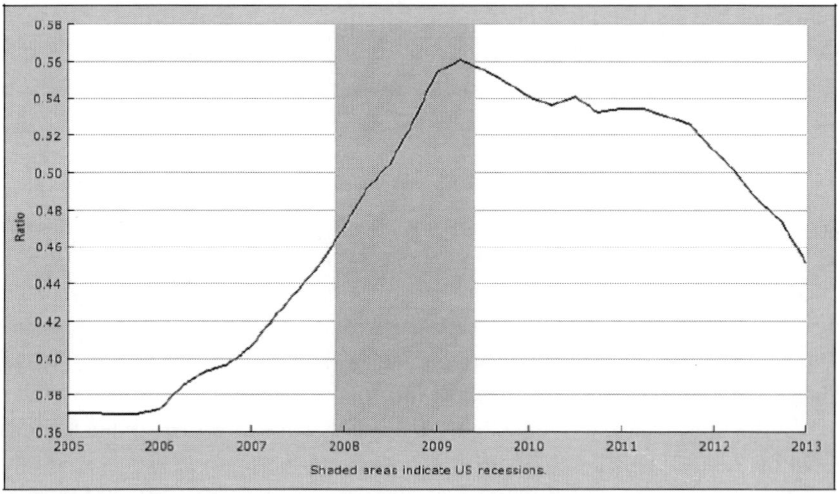

Source: Board of Governors of the Federal Reserve System.

Figure 12. Ratio of Mortgage Debt to Real Estate Assets.

ANY SIGNS CONSUMERS ARE SPENDING MORE FREELY?

A number of indicators paint a mixed picture of the prospect for stronger consumer spending.

- Consumer confidence, as measured by households' attitudes and expectations about their finances, economic conditions and the buying climate has increased to the highest level in six years according to the Thomson Reuters/ University of Michigan Index.[21]
- The Federal Reserve's senior loan officer opinion survey on bank lending practices reported for the fifth consecutive month that the demand for prime residential mortgages had strengthened on net. In

addition, the demand for automobile and credit card loans had strengthened on balance.[22]

- The personal saving rate out of real disposable income in 2012 was 4.1%, down from 5.1% in 2011. In the first quarter of 2013, the personal saving rate decreased to 2.5%. A fall in the saving rate could be an indicator of households turning away from balance sheet repair and toward increased consumption spending. However, the first quarter result could also be a manifestation of lower disposable income caused by the increase in the payroll tax in January. With income down, households may have reached into saving to maintain their level of consumption spending, an action unlikely to be sustainable.[23]
- Real consumer spending in the first half of 2013 increased at an annual rate of 2.0%, slower than the 2.2% pace seen over the previous three years. This rate of spending falls short of what would be needed to accelerate the pace of the recovery (and as noted above may have received a temporary boost from reduced saving). Also, core retail sales for April through June 2013 have slowed relative to the first three months of the year.[24]

POLICY IMPLICATIONS

If household net worth is judged not to have fully recovered from the damage incurred in 2008- 2009, particularly for the typical household, then this would suggest to some a continuing need for macroeconomic policy to provide stimulus to maintain the recovery's upward momentum.

At this point, stimulus from fiscal policy has ended and concerns about long term fiscal imbalance are a barrier to its being reapplied. So the question of continued need relates to monetary policy and when the Federal Reserve could begin to taper its asset purchases associated with its current policy of quantitative easing (commonly referred to as QE3). The Fed has said that a slowing of QE3 is contingent on clear signs of improving economic conditions, particularly labor market conditions. The incomplete repair of the household balance sheet would be one factor suggesting that those clear signs are not likely to appear in the immediate future.[25]

The current state of household net worth, particularly the still large number of households with negative equity in their homes, could also have implications for the continuing need for federal policies such as the Home

Affordable Modification Program (HAMP) that are aimed at providing direct help in removing the burden of household debt through policies that restructure mortgage debt.[26]

End Notes

[1] See CRS Report, Economic Recovery: Sustaining U.S. Economic Growth in a Post-Crisis Economy, by Craig K. Elwell.

[2] Data on real GDP are available from the Department of Commerce, Bureau of Economic Analysis, at http://www.bea.gov/national/index.htm#gdp. Size of output gap is based on the Congressional Research Service (CRS) calculations using Congressional Budget Office (CBO) estimate of potential GDP, data for which is available at FRED Economic Data, St. Louis Fed, at http://research.stlouisfed.org/fred2/series/GDPPOT. Data on unemployment and employment are available from the Department of Labor, Bureau of Labor Statistics, at http://www.bls.gov/.

[3] U.S. Congressional Budget Office, The Effect of Automatic Stabilizers on the Federal Budget as of 2013, March 13, 2013, available at http://www.cbo.gov/publication/43977. In 2011, 2012, and the first half of 2013, the contribution to real GDP growth from spending by the federal government has been negative. See the Department of Commerce, Bureau of Economic Analysis, National Income and Product Accounts, Table 1.1.2, available at http://www.bea.gov/ national/index.htm#gdp.

[4] See CRS Report, Economic Recovery: Sustaining U.S. Economic Growth in a Post-Crisis Economy, by Craig K. Elwell.

[5] Data on wealth and financial flows available at the Board of Governors of the Federal Reserve System, available at http://www.federalreserve.gov/releases/z1/Current/z1r-5.pdf.

[6] U.S. Census Bureau, Houesehold Wealth in the U.S. 2000-2011, available at http://www.census.gov/people/wealth/ files/Wealth%20Highlights%202011.pdf.

[7] Collapse of housing market began before the recession and was a major factor causing the economy-wide collapse.

[8] Case-Shiller Home Price Index-20 City, S&P Dow Jones Indices, available at http://us.spindices.com/index-family/ real-estate/sp-case-shiller.

[9] Karl E. Case, John H. Quigley, and Robert J. Shiller, Wealth Effects Revisited 1975-2012, National Bureau of Economic Research, Working Paper 18667, January 2013, available at http://www.nber.org/papers/w17830.

[10] Karen Dyan, "Is U.S. Household Debt Overhang Holding Back Consumption?" Brookings Papers on Economic Activity, spring 2012, available at http://www.brookings.edu/research /papers/2012/09/debt-overhang-dynan.

[11] Atif Mian and Amir Sufi, What Explains High Unemployment? The Aggregate Demand Channel, National Bureau of Economic Research, Working Paper 17830, February 2012, at http://www.nber.org/papers/w17830.

[12] See Evan Tanner and Yassar Abdih, "Rebuilding U.S. Wealth," Finance & Development, IMF, December 2009 at http://www.imf.org/external/pubs/ft/fandd/2009/12/tanner.htm; and Deniz Igan, Daniel Leigh, John Simon, and Petia Topalova, "Dealing with Household Debt," IMF Global Financial Stability Report, available at http://www.imf.org/ external/np/seminars/eng/2012/fincrises/pdf/ch18.pdf.

[13] Data from Flow of Funds, Z.1. Release, Board of Governors of the Federal Reserve System, available at http://www.federalreserve.gov/releases/z1/Current/z1r-5.pdf.

[14] Date on PCE price index is available at Department of Commerce, Bureau of Economic Analysis, at http://www.bea.gov/national/index.htm#gdp.

[15] See again U.S. Census Bureau, Household Wealth in the U.S. 2000-2011, available at http://www.census.gov/people/ wealth/files/Wealth%20Highlights%202011.pdf.

[16] Zillow Real Estate Research, http://www.zillowblog.com/research/2013/05/22/millions-remain-trapped-by-effectivenegative-equity-in-q1-even-if-theyre-not-underwater/.

[17] See again Case-Shiller Home Price Index-20 City, S&P Dow Jones Indices, available at http://us.spindices.com/ index-family/real-estate/sp-case-shiller.

[18] Meta Brown, Andrew Haughwout, Dongloon Lee, and Wilbert van der Klaauw, "The Financial Crisis at the Kitchen Table: Trends in Household Debt and Credit," Federal Reserve Bank of New York, Current Issues in Economics and Finance, vol. 19, no. 2, 2013, at http://www.newyorkfed.org/research/current_issues/ci19-2.html.

[19] Board of Governors of the Federal Reserve System, Household Debt Service and Financial Obligations Ratios, available at http://www.federalreserve.gov/releases/housedebt /default.htm.

[20] See Karen Dyan, "Is U.S. Household Debt Overhang Holding Back Consumption? Brookings Papers on Economic Activity, spring 2012, available at http://www.brookings.edu/research /papers/2012/09/debt-overhang-dynan.

[21] Surveys of Consumer Confidence, Thomson Reuters/University of Michigan, July 2013, available at http://www.sca.isr.umich.edu/.

[22] The Federal Reserve Board, Senior Loan Officers Opinion Survey on Bank Lending, April 2013, available at http://www.federalreserve.gov/boarddocs/SnLoanSurvey/.

[23] Department of Commerce, Bureau of Economic Analysis, available at http://www.bea.gov/national/index.htm#gdp.

[24] Saving data from Department of Commerce, Bureau of Economic Analysis, available at http://www.bea.gov/ national/index.htm#gdp. Retail sales data from the U.S. Census Bureau, available at http://www.census.gov/retail/.

[25] See CRS Report RL30354, Monetary Policy and the Federal Reserve: Current Policy and Conditions, by Marc Labonte.

[26] See CRS Report R42480, Reduce, Refinance, and Rent? The Economic Incentives, Risks, and Ramifications of Housing Market Policy Options, by Sean M. Hoskins.

INDEX

G

H

I

J

L

M

O

P

R

S

T

U

W